David Steel was born in Scotland in 1938 and was educated in Nairobi, Kenya, and in Edinburgh. He graduated from Edinburgh University with an MA in 1960 and an LL.B in 1962. He was President of the University Liberal Club and of the Students' Representative Council.

He was Assistant Secretary to the Scottish Liberal Party from 1962 to 1964, and became the youngest member of the 1964-66 Parliament when he was elected MP for Roxburgh, Selkirk and Peebles in the by-election of 1965. He was President of the Anti-Apartheid Movement from 1967-70, and he reformed the law on abortion with his Private Member's Bill of 1967.

He has travelled widely throughout the world, is a frequent lecturer in the United States and a regular visitor to African nations.

David Steel was the Liberal Chief Whip from 1970 to 1975, and was elected Leader of the Liberal Party in 1976. He became the youngest Privy Counsellor in 1977. A former TV reporter for BBC Scotland, he is a regular contributor to *The Times*, *The Guardian* and other journals. His pamphlets include 'Boost for the Borders' (1964), 'Out of Control' (1968), 'The Liberal Way Forward' (1975), 'A New Political Agenda' (1976), 'Militant for the Reasonable Man' (1977), 'A New Majority for a New Parliament' (1978) and 'The High Ground of Politics' (1979). He has also written *No Entry: The Background and Implications of the Commonwealth Immigrants Act 1968*.

Weidenfeld and Nicolson
91 Clapham High Street, London SW4

A House Divided

A House Divided

The Lib–Lab Pact and the Future of British Politics

David Steel

Weidenfeld and Nicolson
London

For Judy

Contents

Cartoons		vi
Introduction		vii
1	Political Apprenticeship	1
2	Twice in the Balance	8
3	From MP to Leader	17
4	Towards Lib–Lab	26
5	First Phase of the Agreement, March–June 1977	43
6	The Agreement is Renewed	59
7	The Brighton Conference and the Queen's Speech	77
8	The Great Devolution Debacle	92
9	The Pact in Danger	102
10	The 1978 Budget and the Life of the Pact Draws Quietly to its Close	123
11	Lessons of the Lib–Lab Period	152
12	The Future	158
	Appendices	167
	Index	193

Cartoons

Franklin cartoon in *The Sun*, 25 March 1977   40

Mac cartoon in the *Daily Mail*, 25 March 1977   40

Gibbard cartoon in *The Guardian*, 23 March 1977   41

Franklin cartoon in *The Sun*, 21 July 1977   73

Garland cartoon in the *Daily Telegraph*, 26 May 1978   140

Garland cartoon in the *Daily Telegraph*, 29 June 1978   146

Keith Wate cartoon in the *Sunday Mirror*, 2 July 1978   147

Introduction

'If a house be divided against itself that house cannot stand.'
St Mark's Gospel, Ch. 2

'A house divided against itself cannot stand.'
Abraham Lincoln, 1858

Throughout this book there is the constant theme of the need for parliamentary government to be more broadly based than on one minority political party if it is to be successful. Our industrial, economic and social divisions in Britain are positively encouraged by the pattern of class-based two-party trench warfare which has dominated our national politics for the last thirty years, to the great detriment of our country and her people.

The origins of the book lie in the notes I kept during the Lib–Lab parliamentary pact of 1977–8. I do not keep a diary, but early on in the working agreement I started to write a daily note of my many meetings, formal and informal, in order to be able to keep track of the multiplicity and speed of events in which I found myself involved. This could be described as a temporary diary, though as the reader will discover it has no pretensions to literary merit nor to the discursive style established by Richard Crossman. It is a cryptic record of what actually happened as seen through my eyes.

Official minutes were taken of all formal meetings between Liberals and ministers. Some of these were circulated to those concerned, and I have included a sample both in the text and as appendices. Others – such as the meetings between the Prime Minister and me – were not regularly circulated, though relevant extracts were provided to appropriate ministers from time to time. I assume that these official records will not see the light of day until the fulfilment of the thirty-year rule. Therefore, I repeat, this account is my own version.

One problem I found in selecting from my own notes for

publication was the exercise of self-censorship. Cabinet ministers writing their record of events submit the text for official clearance. But our meetings and papers had no clear status. I therefore wrote to Mr Callaghan when he was still Prime Minister inviting him to examine the text when complete and comment on it. He politely declined. I told him several months after he ceased to be Prime Minister and when the work was far advanced that I was having difficulty in deciding on the propriety of publishing some of our conversations, and repeated the invitation, but again he said he preferred to leave that to my judgement. Now, I know from experience that Jim Callaghan is not exactly an apostle of open government, and he may feel I have been too free in my public account of events. I have in fact held back very little of importance from my notes of what took place, because I believe the way in which our agreement worked is a matter of some constitutional and historic interest. It was a parliamentary but not governmental coalition – a unique experiment.

With the passage of time the original concept of the book has expanded. The core of it remains the working of the Lib–Lab pact, but the first three chapters give my own experience of politics and the thinking which led to the creation of the pact, and the last two give a brief account of the lessons from it and the role of the Liberals in the future.

I am indebted to a large number of people who have helped in compiling this book. To Richard Holme who kept encouraging me to write it, helped construct the format, and also read and commented on the drafts; to John Silverlight of *The Observer* who advised on and edited the sections serialized in that paper in the spring of 1979; to Archy Kirkwood and Andrew Gifford, my political assistants during the period of the Lib–Lab pact; to Rosemary Kirkwood who typed most of my notes and created order out of the chaos of my papers; to my secretary Tessa Horton; to Lynda Sinclair and Nali Dinshaw who struggled with my handwriting to type the text itself; to Andrea Hertz of our whips' office who kept searching her records for answers to my queries; to Nadir Dinshaw, who has over these last years been as an older brother to me; to John Pardoe who also read and commented on the text; to my parliamentary colleagues, party officers and constituency association; to Judy for her support and forbearance both during the events described and the production of the work itself; and likewise to Graeme, Catriona, Rory and Billy.

Chapter 1

Political Apprenticeship

I first developed a serious interest in Liberal politics during the 1959 general election when as President of the Edinburgh University Liberals I made my first public speech to the electorate. (Hitherto it was all just good fun in the cloistered atmosphere of school and university.) I addressed a mammoth audience of about forty in a draughty schoolroom in the South Edinburgh constituency on behalf of William Douglas-Home, the genial playwright, younger brother of Alec. I don't recall what effect I had on the electorate or on him. Suffice it to say that he was not elected and left the Liberal Party shortly afterwards.

But 1959 was a watershed in British politics. It was the 'never had it so good' election in which Harold Macmillan led an ageing and battered Tory cabinet through the post-Suez traumas to a sweeping victory and hence on to complete thirteen years of continuous Conservative government. The Labour Party was demoralized and divided. Hugh Gaitskell's leadership was challenged by the left on two grounds: unilateral disarmament, with which I had some emotional sympathy, and clause four of the Labour Party constitution whose commitment to universal public ownership they were anxious to retain. On that I had no sympathy.

In the 1959-62 period I came to know Jo Grimond well because of his election as Rector of the University, and I worked closely with him as President of the Students' Representative Council. I became committed not just to the man as leader of the Liberal Party but especially to his ideas and his publicly proclaimed vision of a realignment of the left in British politics. Jo was strongly critical of the suffocating complacency of Tory rule both at home and abroad, but like so many was frustrated at the apparent impotence of the Labour Party as a credible alternative.

Jo argued that as long as the present structure of party politics remained unaltered a reactionary Tory Party would tend to prevail.

He was critical of the small 'l' liberals in the Tory Party who attempted to ride on the back of the tiger and always ended up inside it. He wanted to see a truly fundamentalist socialist party and a left of centre radical party which could include the Gaitskellites, leaving a thorough-going Conservative Party on the right. He saw the Liberal Party's role more as the catalyst to bring that about rather than the vehicle to propel him into Number Ten at the head of a Liberal administration. His policy profoundly shocked more traditional Liberals dedicated to a simplistic return of a Liberal Party government, and although the party was devoted to him personally they were suspicious of what one prominent lady described as his 'a-whoring after foreign women'. But Jo was undaunted and during this period attracted a great many fresh minds to revive the ancient corpse of the historic Liberal Party. One of these was John Pardoe, who came over from the Labour Party, though I was not to know him till several years later. Jo's achievement has been underestimated. He took over the leadership of a dying party which in the previous election of 1955 polled 2.7 per cent of the votes and at one point was down to just five MPs (two of them in seats under old 'pact' arrangements and subsequently lost), injected fresh ideas and harnessed the idealism of a whole new generation.

Meantime Gaitskell was conducting his own battle inside the Labour Party. He came to speak at Edinburgh University. I was impressed by his dry but passionate sincerity. He didn't just want power; he knew what he wanted to do with it in the transformation of our society. He was heckled and questioned by the left of his party, but in an orderly manner unlike the semi-riot he endured in Glasgow the following day. At the end of the meeting I met him briefly. My good friend John Mackintosh was present and we adjourned for coffee afterwards. (John was a junior history lecturer of mine at the time. Later he was Labour MP for the neighbouring constituency to mine, Berwick and East Lothian, and Professor of Politics at Edinburgh. But for his untimely death in 1978, he would have written the foreword to this book.) In a television profile of me fifteen years later after I became leader of the Liberal Party he recalled that occasion and suggested that I was close to joining the Labour Party. That was an exaggeration, but it is undoubtedly true that if the Labour Party had been as Gaitskell was, the need for and relevance of the Liberal Party at that time would have been largely eclipsed. But of course it was not to be. Opposed by Harold

Wilson and others he failed to revise the party's constitution and to this day the Labour Party has continued as an unwieldy coalition embodying everything from Marxists to social democrats. On economic issues the Liberals identified with the latter, though sometimes on libertarian issues and such questions as race with some of the left wing.

So in the early 1960s Jo's gospel of 'realignment of the left' gathered momentum. At by-elections the Labour Party in disarray found difficulty in benefiting from the almost inevitable mid-term unpopularity of and swings away from the government. Apart from a fleeting and tenuous victory by Jo's brother-in-law Mark Bonham-Carter in the traditionally fertile Liberal West Country at Torrington in 1958, the Liberals had scored no parliamentary gains at all since 1950. We were stuck with six MPs. But a series of spectacular by-election near-victories led to the astonishing gain by Eric Lubbock of the safe Tory seat at Orpington in 1962. After the death of the former leader Clement Davies, the by-election in Montgomery later in the year returned Emlyn Hooson, the youngest QC of his day. The party sailed towards the forthcoming general election with high hopes.

At this time I had completed my arts and law degrees but had long since abandoned my original intention of going to the Scottish bar, lacking both the legal connections and finance at that time required. Politics was my consuming interest and so I readily accepted the offer in 1962 of a temporary post as assistant secretary to the Scottish Liberal Party at the princely salary of £850 per annum. This was intended to last a year or so until the unknown date of the general election. (In fact after Macmillan's sudden retirement the government lasted unexpectedly the full length of the parliament through to the autumn of 1964.)

At the same time I was already adopted as prospective parliamentary candidate for the Pentlands division of Edinburgh where I had been at school. On this insecure economic basis I got married. We blued our total wealth of £60 on our honeymoon in Skye and set up home in a three-roomed rented house in the constituency. Judy continued to work as a solicitor, and in the evenings we would plod round the doorsteps. We scored one modest success when in the post-Orpington wave the Liberals captured from the Tories one of the four wards in the division on the city council. But in another safe Labour ward the Liberal organization was so sketchy that Judy had to stand as the candidate herself simply to ensure that it was contested at all.

By the end of 1963 I had gained valuable experience of the fundamentals of grassroots politics. I had even acted as deputy agent to the Liberal candidate in the famous Kinross and West Perthshire by-election where the new Prime Minister, having renounced his earldom, sought entry to the Commons. I first met Alec Douglas-Home during the count, where we came a respectable second.

I had been nursing the Pentlands division for two years and had made many friends in the constituency association. But we were under no illusion that the object of the exercise was anything but to save our deposit and if possible head towards 20 per cent of the vote. In my wilder moments I thought a second place perhaps just possible. (In fact the Liberals polled 13.4 per cent there in 1964.) Everyone was anticipating an election in the spring and with only three months to go there was still a vacancy for the Liberal candidature in Roxburgh, Selkirk and Peebles where the Hon. James Tennant, a distant relative of Jo Grimond's, had withdrawn after finding himself and the constituency association mutually incompatible.

The Borders were traditionally Liberal country. Indeed in 1950 the Roxburgh and Selkirk seat was the only one in Scotland apart from Jo's Orkney and Shetland to fall narrowly to the Liberals. It was equally narrowly lost again in 1951. Thereafter the more Tory Peeblesshire had been added to it and by 1959 it had become a fairly safe Tory seat with a majority of nearly 10,000. But the Liberals still had just held second place against a vigorous campaign by the Labour candidate Tam Dalyell. Labour had always been third, though in 1945 were within 2,000 of victory with the Liberals sandwiched in the middle. Now we were in danger of losing our hold on second place in the seat.

The party hierarchy determined that an adequate candidate should be shifted from some less promising seat to this one. The local Liberals made overtures to one who found his own constituency up in arms at the suggestion and therefore backed out. My name was then proposed and I decided after some initial hesitation that the right thing to do was to switch, even though this meant abandoning two years of effort in Pentlands. George Mackie (later MP for Caithness and Sutherland and now Lord Mackie of Benshie) assisted in the process as chairman of the party's organization committee and had a vote of censure passed on him by the Scottish Party Executive for his pains.

I was adopted for the Roxburgh, Selkirk and Peebles constituency in January 1964. Fate then took a hand with Sir Alec's announcement that he would continue the government through to the autumn. Instead of fighting a strange constituency in the spring, we gave up our house in Edinburgh in May and moved to the Borders. Our summer holiday was devoted to visiting every hamlet in the unique three-county constituency as well as getting to know industry in the eight burghs. At nights I attended an endless series of social and political functions. It all paid off and in the general election the Tory majority was reduced from nearly 10,000 to under 2,000 with the Labour vote also reduced a couple of thousand.

Three of the four Liberal gains in that election were in Scotland. The party's UK vote was 11.2 per cent, an improvement on 1959's 5.9 per cent but still a disappointment after the Orpington era. The Border seat could now be regarded as 'winnable' again and with the new Labour government having a majority of only three the next election was unlikely to be as far away as five years.

I duly left my post in the Scottish party HQ and signed a six-month contract to be a presenter/reporter in the TV current affairs department of BBC Scotland. This would mean travelling once or twice a week to Glasgow but it meant I could stay in the Borders and keep my name before the electorate until such time as the next election occurred. In mid-December, just two months after the election, I was recording the regular weekly programme when the producer told me that the MP for Roxburgh, Selkirk and Peebles had died in a London hospital while undergoing a routine operation. I thought he was playing a practical joke until he went next door to the newsroom and produced the piece of paper which the newsreader had just been using.

This meant an unexpected by-election which we were well placed to win. I doubted whether there was all that much further swing available from the Tories and decided that we should concentrate on a further squeeze of the Labour vote. The Borders, I thought, should be a test case for realignment. Only in 1959 had the Tories an overall majority against Liberal and Labour added together. Now a realignment of those two forces would itself be sufficient to put them out.

Over the Christmas and New Year period I happened to bump

into Ronald King Murray in Edinburgh. He had been the Labour candidate in the election. (He later became MP for the Leith division of Edinburgh and Lord Advocate in the 1974–9 Labour government.) 'I hope,' I said, 'you're not going to stand in the by-election.' My reason was that he was rather too strong a candidate for my liking and totally wasted in such a forlorn battle for Labour. We had a short discussion in which he made it clear that he would feel duty bound to stand again if he were asked. This came as a disappointment since I thought it would make my task more difficult. 'I'm afraid you'll have to lose your deposit if I am going to win' was my parting advice. In the campaign which followed that is exactly what happened. The Labour vote fell to 11.3 per cent. In the course of two campaigns in six months I persuaded nearly half the Labour voters to switch to me.

The process was helped by the style of the Tory campaign. They adopted Robin McEwen of Marchmont, Etonian heir to the baronetcy in Berwickshire. I never met him during the campaign except to shake hands formally and it was not till a couple of years afterwards that in conversation he struck me as both agreeable and able. Somehow this never came across in the campaign. Instead, unused to being heckled, he tended to lose his temper. I'm afraid that when this became known little bands of my supporters went round his meetings provoking him and most therefore ended in disaster with visiting Tory leaders such as Keith Joseph sitting head buried in hands on the platform. The Borders is one of the few constituencies where public meetings still matter. We had about fifty each, attended by truly massive audiences. Indeed George Brown in three meetings on one evening addressed almost as many as the 4,936 people who actually voted Labour.

Just about every member of the Tory shadow cabinet appeared. (Except for the leader, Sir Alec, who adhered to the tradition of not appearing yet suffered the blame and found the loss of the seat used as a lever against him. He resigned three months later.) The local chain of newspapers, owned by a jolly lieutenant-colonel from New Zealand of impeccable right-wing Tory views, made the great mistake of backing McEwen and publishing a massive feature on his stately home. This merely served further to alienate the populace. Our canvassers were instructed to woo the Labour voters. This was done so successfully that tales reached us of Labour canvassers on the council estates giving up in disgust and actually canvassing for me rather than waste their day out from Glasgow or wherever.

The late John Bannerman (later Lord Bannerman of Kildonan), then chairman of the Scottish Liberal Party, dubbed me 'the boy David' against the Goliath might of the Tories. The epithet stuck and was used in the *Daily Express* front-page headline the day after the poll: 'It's boy David!'. I entered the House of Commons as its youngest member on 28 March 1965, three days before my twenty-seventh birthday. 'Realignment' had produced a surprisingly large Liberal majority of over 4,000. The Labour candidate's wife, discomfited by their lost deposit, was asked whether she wasn't all the same pleased at the Tory defeat. 'Not at all,' she replied, 'it confuses the class war.'

Chapter 2

Twice in the Balance

In the summer of 1965, the Labour government was struggling along on its majority of three. Before my entry at the by-election there had been one official approach from a member of the cabinet to the Liberal parliamentary party for support in one vital vote. The Liberals had refused this not so much on the merits of the argument – it was an aviation question – but for fear of being identified as saviours of the Labour Party. Some members of the party, with hindsight, argue that this was the first significant time that the Liberals failed to appreciate the potential use of a new balance of power in the Commons. At any rate the matter passed without any great attention being paid to it.

But then the role of the Liberals was thrown into sharp relief and debate with the sudden death during the summer recess of the Speaker, Sir Harry Hylton-Foster. He had been a Conservative and he had two deputies, one Labour, one Tory. The Tories promptly decided that they would not supply a replacement. This meant Labour producing one from their own ranks and reducing their precious majority to two.

At this point the government decided to encourage press speculation that a Liberal might be appropriate for the job. At this suggestion the party first demonstrated to me an endearing but infuriating lack of discipline. They behaved like a flock of flapping chickens in a hen run at the appearance of a fox. Various individuals and parts of the party in the country started conveying public advice against having anything to do with such a notion. Peter Bessell, MP for Bodmin, appeared on television in Plymouth ('I thought it was only being shown in the West Country,' he said afterwards with breathtaking naïvety) proposing that Jo Grimond should be Speaker. This was then relayed on national news and in next day's newspapers. I have never seen Jo in such a fury as he was after that episode.

By the time the parliamentary party assembled in London a specific government approach had been made to Roderic Bowen QC, the Liberal MP for Cardigan. If he would accept nomination, Labour would not back one of their own number and the Tories were refusing to nominate one of theirs. Bowen was clearly keen to have the job but nobody else seemed willing for him to have it except possibly his Welsh colleague Emlyn Hooson and myself as the new boy. I saw some merit in his taking it. Bowen was the senior member of the parliamentary party, having been elected in 1945. He had had therefore a twenty-year innings as a backbencher. Though both clever and witty, he was busy at the bar and thus we rarely saw him, nor did he any longer take an active role in the party in the country. I did not believe therefore that his elevation to the Speakership would be felt as an irreparably grievous loss to the party. There would be some prestige for the party in the appointment and more importantly he could end Hylton-Foster's policy of ignoring the Liberals' rights as a party in the House. (In fairness, this was in fact put right by the three following Speakers.)

The failure to back Bowen was partly his own fault. He was asked at least twice whether, if he were not elected Speaker, he would accept appointment as one of the deputies (these not being subject to open election in the same way). To this he refused to give a straight answer. If he had said 'yes', that might have persuaded his colleagues that it would be better in that case to back him for the main job. As it was he could not be nominated as Speaker if his own party opposed, and the House elected Dr Horace King as Labour's nominee. Bowen was then appointed as deputy Speaker, thus preserving the government's majority, reducing our voting power by one, and missing the political opportunity of establishing close goodwill and liaison between us and the Labour government. Bowen suffered all the disadvantage of being in the Chair with none of the advantages, including the clear run at election, and he lost his seat in the March 1966 election. Such is the ingratitude of politics that he was never rewarded by Labour by so much as elevation to the Lords.

The Liberals therefore suffered indignity and gained nothing out of the fracas. Harold Wilson dissolved parliament six months later, gained an overall majority of nearly a hundred, and our poll was down from 11.2 per cent to 8.6 per cent though we had a net gain of two more seats. With twelve MPs the Liberals now had the biggest parliamentary party since 1945 and found themselves irrelevant. Realignment was further away than ever and we had no leverage on events in the Commons. Although I was unaware of it, Jo indicated to one or two senior colleagues that he wished to resign the leadership, but was persuaded to stay on. But he was clearly fed up. To use his phrase, our teeth were no longer 'in the real meat of power'. They had turned out to be false and apt to fall out when it came to chewing a particularly difficult piece.

In January 1967 Judy and I went to Orkney, my first visit as an MP to the leader's constituency. We took our baby, Graeme, and stayed the weekend with the Grimonds in their old manse where I'd stayed once before as a student. Jo took me into his study before the evening speaking engagement and told me he had decided to resign the leadership of the party and that he thought he had better tell me in case I launched into embarrassing eulogies of his permanent leadership. He would tell his constituency officers over the weekend and the parliamentary party during the week.

I was absolutely shattered, having no inkling that this was about to happen. Nevertheless we discussed the situation calmly. I had been brought into politics by Jo. He had worked imaginatively to promote realignment. That had been knocked on the head by the return of a majority Labour government. After ten years he was tired of trundling round the country appearing in the same town halls with the same message. In the party's interest it was time for fresh leadership and a new direction. There was no point in arguing. I had further engagements in Orkney on the Monday while Jo went back to London to prepare the announcement. In the swift leadership election among the Liberal MPs, Jeremy Thorpe was elected by six votes to three each for Eric Lubbock and Emlyn Hooson.

It was the end of an era, and the next five years, 1967–72, were undramatic ones for the Liberals. In the 1970 general election we lost half our dozen seats and indeed three of us – Jeremy Thorpe, John Pardoe and myself – only survived by three-figure majorities in our own constituencies. We had no very clear message except the assumption of innate virtue and superiority in a host of Liberal policies.

During this frustrating period I threw myself into a series of political activities on an all-party basis. In 1966–7 I had been lucky in drawing a high place in the ballot for private members' Bills. I decided to make the seventh Commons attempt to reform the law on abortion in which the lead had already been given by the House of Lords. This brought me as a junior backbencher into sudden and close contact with senior ministers and plunged me willy-nilly into grasping all the complexities of parliamentary procedure.

Roy Jenkins at the Home Office, Kenneth Robinson at the Ministry of Health, Dick Crossman as Leader of the House and John Silkin as chief whip were all keen supporters. But the reform was highly controversial and aroused strong opposition. The Abortion Act only made it on to the statute book because of the close co-operation of a small band of MPs of all parties. In particular Peter Jackson, the Labour MP for High Peak, and Sir George Sinclair, Conservative MP for Dorking, organized the necessary voting support from the larger parties, especially during the all-night sittings at report stage. I took charge of the committee stage with three junior ministers sitting alongside me. There was constant consultation on what amendments to accept and what to reject.

Because of the delaying tactics of the Bill's opponents I had to ask for a second day and night of government time. I went to see Crossman in the Leader of the House's room which years later I was to know so well. He gave me a generous whisky and poured himself a brandy. He explained in headmasterly but friendly terms that I had not so far made a brilliant job of getting the Bill through and that I had allowed too many changes in committee. He was doubtful whether the cabinet would agree to providing still more time. The Prime Minister was not enthusiastic. As the minutes ticked by I said that if the Bill failed the issue would be bound to return to haunt the government session after session. He agreed to recommend that the necessary time be provided to enable the House to dispose of the Bill one way or the other. He absent-mindedly poured some of his bottle of brandy into the remains of my glass of whisky. I drank the revolting mixture and fled nervously but gratefully from his presence. When the Act received the Royal Assent, Roy Jenkins gave a small party at the Treasury, where he by then had been moved, for all who had worked so hard at seeing the long overdue reform through. It was my first experience of effective cross-party co-operation.

In 1968 the government decided to introduce a quick Bill to stop the entry of British passport-holders from East Africa into Britain. It was a monstrous measure depriving people of their basic rights of citizenship. It increased the panic flood from East Africa over a few days and, as Amin's expulsion of Asians from Uganda later proved, it was largely ineffective. Since I have written a book on the subject this is no place for detailed repetition.* Because of my four years at school in Nairobi I was one of few MPs who understood the position of the British-Asian community there. I was strongly opposed to the Bill, as was the Liberal Party as a whole. While there were dissident Labour and Tory MPs also opposed (notably the former Colonial Secretary Iain Macleod) it needed the Liberal Party to act as the mechanism for opposing and seeking to amend the Bill. Some sixty MPs joined us in the exercise. While on this occasion we were unsuccessful, a close camaraderie emerged among that body prepared to stay through two nights and vote at every opportunity on something to which we all felt strongly opposed.

Just before this I succeeded Barbara Castle and David Ennals as President of the all-party Anti-Apartheid Movement in Great Britain. They had each in turn been elevated to ministerial office, and doubtless the Movement felt safe from such repeated disruption by electing a Liberal. In any case there were hardly any Tories active in it. The three or four years in which I presided over the work of the Movement were rewarding and enjoyable in making common cause with others for a specific and vital purpose.

Further experience of the same phenomenon was provided by my chairmanship of the Scottish Committee of Shelter, the highly successful housing charity and pressure group. Here was all-party work in literally concrete action, and it was particularly gratifying to visit people rehoused in improved conditions by voluntary associations dependent on Shelter's work.

In all of this I was devoting more time and effort to political work outside the limiting confines of the Liberal Party. I held no office in the party and was, not unfairly, criticized for turning my energies to other uses. I used to argue in return that I was keeping an active Liberal presence elsewhere in pursuit of Liberal causes.

After the debacle of the 1970 election and the loss among others of Eric Lubbock, Jeremy Thorpe appointed me chief whip in his place without any great enthusiasm either on the party's part or mine. With a flock of only six the parliamentary role was not burdensome, but there were a lot of party chores which I carried out I suppose competently but not outstandingly.

* *No Entry – The Background and Implications of the Commonwealth Immigrants Act, 1968*, published by C. Hurst & Co., 1969.

Then in 1972 – ten years after Orpington – things began to improve. Again a Tory government was reaching mid-term unpopularity and the Labour Party was failing to gain the advantage of it. Cyril Smith won the Rochdale by-election. I did not know him but I had been in correspondence with him, urging him as an ex-Labour mayor of Rochdale to stand for the constituency now that he had returned to the Liberal fold. This was followed by an upturn in the opinion polls and our gain of the safe Tory seat of Sutton and Cheam. 'Another Orpington' explained all the commentators. Two more gains were recorded on the same day in 1973 at Ripon by David Austick and the Isle of Ely where Clement Freud was the fairly last-minute candidate. Finally in the autumn of 1973 Alan Beith narrowly won the Berwick upon Tweed seat which I had been helping to nurse just across the border through the summer.

This was a much bigger tidal wave of success than the Orpington period where we had had a series of near-misses rather than actual gains. By the winter of 1973 inflation was threatening to rocket out of control. The Tory government, having dismantled Labour's prices and incomes board, had done a complete *volte face* and established new prices and incomes machinery which we supported with some dismay as we had consistently backed the previous one and opposed its abolition. But the damage had been done. A mini-budget was announced for December which failed to take counter-inflationary action. Meantime a series of exorbitant wage claims were made culminating in the miners' strike. This was backed by the Labour opposition and we watched the process of adversative politics at its destructive worst.

The Tory government went to the country in February 1974 with the Liberals rating 12 per cent in the Gallup Poll. The cumulative effect of the by-election gains had been however to raise both party morale and expectations. There were over five hundred Liberal candidates compared with over three hundred in 1970. We polled an astonishing 19.3 per cent compared with 7.5 per cent at the previous election. Jeremy Thorpe led the party in a brilliantly effective campaign largely conducted by closed-circuit television from his own marginal seat. Our poll ratings rose steadily during the campaign to the point where in his final broadcast Jeremy was persuaded by some in the party to make a direct appeal for the return of a Liberal government, a highly incredible prospect which may have caused the slight drop in actual support by polling day. But the cruel blow was that despite going into the election with eleven MPs and hoping for many more, we had a net gain of only three seats to show for our six million votes. The unfairness of the election system was demonstrated to us more clearly than ever before. The Tories had polled 11,900,000 votes to Labour's 11,700,000; however, Labour had secured four more seats than the Tories. But they were seventeen short of an overall majority.

The Liberal Party was totally unprepared for what happened next. On the Friday after polling day Prime Minister Heath sent for the leader of the Liberal Party. Jeremy Thorpe took the next train from Devon to London, and once again the party was rattled. Unsolicited, contrary and public advice again poured in from all directions. The public picture was one of disarray for which, with the benefit of hindsight, Jeremy accepts some portion of blame since he had told no one what he was doing. I as chief whip heard about it on the car radio.

Heath told him that since no one had an overall majority and he (Heath) had more votes than Wilson he proposed to stay on if Liberals would support him with perhaps a seat in the cabinet. Jeremy pointed out that he also had a grievance about the system. With six million votes – half as many as the others – we had only fourteen MPs. He asked Heath to consider the case for electoral reform.

On Saturday evening I flew to London and talked to Jeremy. It seemed to me that the case against accepting Heath's proposal was overwhelming: 1. Tories and Liberals together still had no majority. The new Ulster members were the Paisleys and Powells, not, as before, aligned Tories. 2. Heath himself had decided to go to the country, and had lost his majority. 3. The big Liberal vote was largely against the Tories' incapacity to deal with a worsening economic and industrial situation, and it would be odd now to throw that weight behind him. Nevertheless if the injustice of the election system could be put right we should not turn it down out of hand.

I drove with Jeremy for a second meeting at Downing Street and waited in the car in the dark by the back entrance for the half-hour he was talking to the Prime Minister. When he returned he said that all that was on offer was a Speaker's Conference to consider electoral reform. Since we had had many such before we considered this fairly useless.

On Sunday Jeremy had publicly invited Jo, myself and Frank

Byers as leader of the Liberal peers and elder statesman of the party to lunch at his house to discuss the Heath offer. While this was not unreasonable it infuriated much of the rest of the party inside and outside parliament who assumed, and were egged on by the press to assume, that some deal was being concocted. In fact we decided that we could not recommend acceptance of the proposal to our colleagues.

MPs began drifting to London for discussion on Sunday, and we met formally to decide and announce our view on Monday. There was a last-minute dispute over whether we would admit the peers to our discussion. There are nominally over thirty of them, some of them rare attenders and unknown quantities, others very hard working and valuable substitutes for our mere handful of MPs. It was decided that Byers would represent them and the rest were sent somewhat ungraciously packing.

Early in the discussion it became clear that the almost universal view was that we should not go into a Heath government. However, in the course of the argument one theme kept recurring on which Jo Grimond, Russell Johnston, MP for Inverness, and I expressed anxiety, namely the proposition that it was quite wrong ever to consider collaboration of this kind with any other party. We pointed out that it was nonsense for a party which believed in proportional representation not to be willing in principle to work with others, and that we should be prepared in the right circumstances (which these admittedly were not) to do so to secure progress to electoral reform and the processes of realigning and reforming the party political structure. But we were a minority and in any case agreed this was not that opportunity.

The party endorsed a statement drafted by Jeremy urging Heath to consider talking to Wilson and himself about the formation of a government of national recovery. If, however, he wished simply to continue with his minority Conservative government in office we would be prepared to consider giving support from the opposition benches to an agreed programme in the national interest. This last was in fact precisely the same offer we subsequently made to Prime Minister Callaghan, but it later suited Tory propagandists to pretend crudely that we turned the Tories down but accepted Labour's offer.

After consulting his cabinet colleagues Prime Minister Heath decided not to pursue either of these avenues but to resign. He drove to Buckingham Palace to surrender the seals of office, to be followed closely by Harold Wilson driving to pick them up.

Over the weekend I had telephoned Roy Jenkins on my own initiative to inquire whether he thought there were any possibility of a Lib–Lab arrangement of the sort we had proposed to Heath to form a more secure government. He said rightly that he thought Wilson would not contemplate this and would simply form a minority Labour government and, as in 1964–6, look for the earliest chance to turn it into a big majority one.

It seemed to me as we settled in to the new parliament that history was in danger of repeating itself after ten years: Liberal by-election success, disappointment at the general election, failure to co-operate with a fragile Labour government, the election of a secure Labour government, and a further period of irrelevance and decline for the Liberal Party. Prospects for that elusive realignment seemed again dim, but the party's internal convulsions at the mere offer from Heath made me convinced that so long as we kept dodging such questions and simply pretending to be an alternative government in exile we would continue to fail.

Chapter 3

From MP to Leader

The reverberations of the Heath/Thorpe talks continued through all organs of the party over the next four months of 1974 until at the end of June I was summing up a television party political broadcast in which our three new MPs Paul Tyler (Bodmin), Stephen Ross (Isle of Wight) and Geraint Howells (Cardigan) appeared. In words strangely prescient of my approach in 1979 I said as chief whip:

> I only wish that the voting system had given us more members like these. But did you realize that the present Labour government represents less than a third of the total electorate? Now, we Liberals – unlike the other parties – are not saying vote for us because we alone have all the answers. We believe that the Liberal Party can contribute some of the answers; but there is a growing public conviction that the fight against inflation cannot be successfully waged by any government narrowly based on one party appealing to one sectional interest in our community. In our crisis we surely need a much more broadly based government, backed by a real majority of public opinion and that means that all parties must be willing to come together on an agreed programme in the national interest.
>
> I find the public demand for a government of national unity is now gaining considerable force but it can only come about if we get more Liberals in parliament. We are ready and willing to participate in such a government if at the next election you give us the power to do so. Naturally, like the other parties, we'd prefer you to give us an overall majority of seats, but if you don't we remain ready to contribute towards the kind of fair government based on partnership which you – the electorate – might be seeking. Any party which refused to consider this would be seeking to put power for their own party before the will of the people.

After the last election we rejected Mr Heath's invitation to join a government under him because a coalition between 290 Conservatives and only 14 Liberals would have been just a Tory government in disguise but in any case such a combination would have lacked the necessary majority in the House of Commons.

The pattern of the two-party stranglehold on British politics is breaking up. That has not been achieved by politicians; you have done it. You have decided rightly that it must end. And what we Liberals ask of you now is that at the next election, whenever it comes, you give us sufficient members in parliament to ensure the end of the system of one-party government which has failed in recent years to unite the nation and give our country the kind of reforming government which represents the wishes of a clear majority of our people and which alone will therefore have the capacity to solve our problems.

Although Jeremy had telephoned me during the recording and required a slight toning down of the original script, it had his approval, but it set the fox among the chickens again. The broadcast was a success in publicity terms and public reaction. Indeed it finally triggered ex-Navy Minister Christopher Mayhew to cross the floor of the Commons from the Labour benches and join us, which in turn further boosted attention to the Liberal cause. But in the party executive and council the grumbles continued against this approach.

Most of the MPs, however, agreed that it should be pursued aggressively. A Liberal balance could be projected as an attainable attraction for the inevitable second election expected at any time. In September the party met in conference at Brighton. The pre-election atmosphere pervaded the assembly and Jeremy Thorpe wisely decided to open the conference with a leader's address to give it some direction rather than wait for the traditional wind-up on the Saturday.

Speeches cannot be written by committees, and in any case the leader's speech always falls after a period of the summer recess when he has been separated from his colleagues. They are therefore not usually consulted on its contents. Each leader tends to gather round him a small group of trusted advisers who think along the same lines, who feed him with ideas and reaction from the party, and off whom he can bounce ideas of his own. In this case he was expected to resolve what was crudely known as the 'coalition question'. I expected him to proclaim a solid election line of seeking wider co-operation in politics with Liberals as the catalyst. Instead he was advised, possibly correctly, not to risk a row in the party on election eve. The result was an acute disappointment to me. In his only reference to the subject he left the distinct impression that if fire, flood and pestilence were to strike the country all at once then the Liberals might just be persuaded to assist in dealing with the disaster. Otherwise we were on our own, our policies so much better, etc., etc. In his wind-up speech at the end of the conference he said of the coming election: 'Our objective will be nothing less than a total breakthrough.'

The assembly was followed by the pre-election hovercraft tour of the coastal resorts in which Jeremy and the appropriate constituency MPs would bring the message to the masses on the beaches. It was a typically original idea of Jeremy's into which he flung himself with gusto. It was not his fault that it ended in the disaster of mockery in atrocious weather. The vessel was filmed and photographed flooded on a deserted beach. But the real complaint came from John Pardoe who observed that while a lot of planning had gone into the tour the one thing never considered was what they were supposed to be actually saying to the people.

The October election campaign was therefore merely a slightly less successful re-run of February. We dropped, despite an extra hundred candidates, from 19.3 per cent to 18.4 per cent of the total vote. We went into it with fifteen MPs and emerged with thirteen, and since Harold Wilson had secured his overall majority we also drifted downward in the opinion polls and at by-elections in our refound irrelevance.

I felt I had now had long enough as party whip and wished to be free of that tying and at times trying responsibility, but there was no obvious successor and so I agreed to stay on a bit longer. By the spring of 1975 forces were gathering for the coming referendum on Britain's 'renegotiated terms' for joining the European Community. I was invited to be the Liberal representative on the all-party 'yes' committee called 'Britain in Europe'. By the summer it had been agreed I should quit as Liberal chief whip and Cyril Smith would take my place. I would become the party's foreign affairs spokesman and so my place in the referendum committee was sensible.

The Liberals had pioneered Britain's membership of the Community and I thought it important that we should take an active part. But the other parties had superior resources at their disposal and more to contribute in men and materials. They were also wary of such dangerous Liberal notions as close political integration following direct elections and preferred to play down future developments. Nevertheless the committee was an exciting place to be, under the presidency of Roy Jenkins with the active participation of the Tory deputy leader Willie Whitelaw, and ex-leaders Ted Heath and Jo Grimond together with several current ministers. It was backed by a small group of powerful ex-Tory Central Office and ex-Transport House mandarins who brought their joint experience of actually winning general elections together.

Before the organization was officially launched the inner group met clandestinely over breakfast at 8.30am. The very idea appalled me since I rarely function well before 10am though am happy to meet through midnight if necessary. However my initial shock at working in such conditions was overcome by the location. Extensive breakfasts of great magnificence were provided in a penthouse suite at the Dorchester by the then owner of the hotel who was a keen supporter. Throughout, the campaign had no difficulty in raising cash and hiring quality employees. The basic materials which Liberals scratched hard to find or finance simply appeared at the flick of fingers: cars, aeroplanes, helicopters, film units, stage equipment, photocopiers, typewriters.

The expertise and contact network of the two big party machines was a real eye-opener to someone used to the poverty-stricken organization of the Liberal Party. When the campaign was officially launched I represented the Liberals in a number of large city-centre rallies, usually as the warmer-upper for the big two billed for the evening. These were immensely successful and enjoyable events, and trailing round the country in this cause enabled me to get on closer terms with senior figures in the other parties.

My activity also revealed a difference with John Pardoe. He was, with some justification, scornful of the 'lowest common denominator' approach of the all-party organization to Europe, and took himself off to the West Country to preach the pure gospel of the Liberal vision of a federal Europe. I was not, however, wholly unsuccessful in slipping appropriate bits into my speeches without too much protest from my Labour and Tory colleagues. I also appeared in a good many television programmes and at press conferences during the campaign.

The result was a resounding victory for the pro-Europeans and in the heady celebrations afterwards there was much loose talk of keeping the politicians of the centre together. The main weakness of the 'antis' had been their composition of too many of Labour's left wing and the Tories' right wing. If sane men of goodwill had attracted such an effective unified response, could this not be pursued in other areas of politics? It sounded attractive but there was no other specific cause awaiting and with the departure of Roy Jenkins to Brussels the committee quietly disbanded. But once again I had been involved in successful co-operation with other parties in pursuit of a Liberal objective.

In the autumn and winter of 1975 I made regular visits to conferences and meetings overseas. The 1975 Liberal assembly at Scarborough was a low-key affair with growing mutterings against the leadership and continuing uncertainty about our direction as a party. After it I spent a fascinating week at the Labour Party conference to comment on it for the BBC *Tonight* programme. It was useful to observe at first hand the workings of This Great Movement of Ours (Tigmoo, as Alan Watkins has christened it). Then in early 1976 Jeremy Thorpe was hit by the double blow of the report on London and County Securities of which he had been a director and the allegations of Norman Scott. He eventually resigned the leadership in March. It could not have come at a more awkward time because the party was in one of its bouts of constitutional change (a harmless activity in which it engages from time to time) and had not yet completed the process of deciding how in future to elect the leader. The party was very critical of the process of election exclusively by a small band of MPs. Jo Grimond was recalled to the temporary leadership while this was sorted out at a special conference in Manchester. A sensible system was agreed whereby the MPs controlled the nominations and the constituencies voted for the candidates. John Pardoe had announced his intention of standing soon after Jeremy resigned. I hesitated because I wanted to discuss it with my family and constituency officials. The chance to announce my intention of putting my hat in the ring came on 18 May at a meeting I was due to address in Hampstead, where ironically the Pardoes live. I began my speech by saying that we should use the debate on new leadership 'to undertake some fundamental reappraisal, not of the content of our policies, but of our priorities and strategy'. I continued:

> The role of the Liberal Party is not that of a shadow third government with a detailed policy on every single issue of the day, ready and waiting in the wings for a shift in electoral opinion to sweep us into power. That is the role of Her Majesty's Opposition, and we are nowhere near that position yet. Our task is a very different one. It is to spell out a clear vision of the society we want to achieve; to provide long-term goals to a people weary of the politics of pragmatism, expediency and compromise.
>
> We must concentrate less on giving day-to-day commentary on the policies of others, and far more on setting out our own programme. And we should combine our long-term programme with a readiness to work with others wherever we see what Jo Grimond has called the break in the clouds – the chance to implement any of Liberal policies. In my political lifetime I have worked closely with those of other parties to promote certain causes: Europe, anti-apartheid, legislation on social reforms, housing, devolution, and electoral reform. The experience has not made me less of a Liberal, not compromised the independence of Liberalism. There are occasionally small 'l' liberals to be found on particular issues outside the Liberal Party, and we should never fear to co-operate with them effectively to promote some part of our cause. As Edmund Burke said: 'When bad men combine, the good must associate, else they will fall one by one, an unpitied sacrifice in a contemptible struggle.'

And I concluded by declaring my candidacy for the leadership:

> It is by now a well-worn political saying that if you can't stand the heat you should get out of the kitchen. In these days it has been put to me bluntly that if you find yourself in the kitchen anyway you might as well take charge of the menu. And so, bearing in mind that the rules for the nomination of candidates are not yet finalized, I feel that I ought to make it clear that in the coming weeks it is my intention to seek candidature for the leadership of our party.
>
> The task for the Liberal Party is nothing less than a repudiation of the tedious repetitive slanging match which passes for

political debate today in and out of the House of Commons. Our role is to renew hope that a more tolerant, a more fair, a more caring, a more open society is within our capacity to create. Let us appeal to those outside our party to come and join us. Let us proclaim with conviction that it is only within the Liberal Party that the aspirations of millions who have long since abandoned all hope and faith in representative politics can be met.

The leadership election campaign itself lasted about three weeks. It was difficult mainly because John Pardoe and I had no basic disagreements on policy or philosophy. It was not like the Labour leadership election a few months earlier where different candidates represented different actual views.

With us the differences lay merely in personality, style and strategy for the party. These were not easy to debate publicly. I stuck to my Hampstead speech line which John effectively tried to undermine in such telling phrases as 'he's too fond of breakfast with Roy Jenkins' or 'he's never out of a dinner jacket'. John was all for the hell-fire blockbusting approach to leading a minority party, and he may well have scared the wits out of some Liberals. But there was no great debate and it was not a particularly enlightening contest even though we exhausted ourselves to the great participatory enjoyment of the party.

On 7 July I was announced the victor by about two to one during a tedious count in which the result was obvious from the start. We both made suitable speeches. Parliament ran another three weeks and then broke for the long summer recess. During this I decided to make a detailed policy speech to my first party assembly as leader in September. When we gathered at Llandudno I had been working on it at home for weeks. I decided also to use my new authority as democratically elected leader to face the 'coalition question' head on. I came to North Wales with my draft text and showed it to one or two people who paled visibly. Then John Pardoe arrived in my suite for a private chat. He had been in Cornwall all summer and I in Scotland without contact. I was fearful lest he had decided either publicly or privately to abandon politics. Instead he told me quietly that the party could have only one leader and one strategy. I had been elected and therefore he would back mine. I should go right ahead.

I was very moved by this because we had had a couple of ferocious private rows during the leadership election. He had been his own worst enemy but I had been less than kind to him. I was deeply grateful because we agreed that by sticking together now we might be able to achieve something. In addition I relied almost entirely on his economic expertise.

Thus emboldened I prepared my final text, only to find that the reaction to the feelers my entourage had put out about what I might say had caused them to have second thoughts. Was it not reckless to risk my first speech in this way? This on the very evening of the speech. It might be wiser to remove the offending passage and argue the case another day. 'Let's go for a walk and clear our heads,' I suggested. Three or four of us went out through the inevitable parties in the hotel foyer and walked along the sea-front park in the dusk. Twenty minutes later we returned. 'It stays in,' I said.

The speech was a good one, but far too long. Televised live, it caused the cancellation of two minor programmes and disappeared abruptly on ITV at 12.30 prompt in favour of *World of Sport*. I was appallingly nervous and the atmosphere was tense. Three-quarters of the way through I reached the difficult part:

> We are in being as a political party to form a government so as to introduce the policies for which we stand. That is our clear aim and objective. But I as leader have a clear obvious duty to assess how most speedily we can reach that objective. I do not expect to lead just a nice debating society.
>
> If we argue that we alone can be the means of transforming the sterility of British political life, if we tell the public that only by voting Liberal in sufficient numbers to prevent one other party gaining a majority, will we achieve electoral reform, and break the Tory/Labour stranglehold, then equally we must be clear in our own minds that if the political conditions are right [which of course they were not in February 1974], and if our own values are retained, we shall probably have – at least temporarily – to share power with somebody else to bring about the changes we seek.
>
> Of course neither of the other parties will want to relinquish their exclusive alternating hold on power, but if the people won't let them have it then they will both have to lump it – Tory and Labour.

I want the Liberal Party to be the fulcrum and centre of the next election argument – not something peripheral to it. If that is to happen we must not give the impression of being afraid to soil our hands with the responsibilities of sharing power.

We must be bold enough to deploy the coalition case positively. We must go all out to attack the other parties for wanting power exclusively to themselves no matter on how small a percentage of public support.

If people want a more broadly based government they must vote Liberal to get it. And if they vote Liberal we must be ready to help provide it.

What I am saying is that I want the Liberals to be an altogether tougher and more determined force. I want us to be a crusading and campaigning movement, not an academic think-tank nor minority influence nor occasional safety valve in the political system.

The road I intend us to travel may be a bumpy one, and I recognize therefore the risk that in the course of it we may lose some of the passengers, but I don't mind so long as we arrive at the end of it reasonably intact and ready to achieve our goals.

None of us in this party is interested in office for office's sake. If we were we would never have joined the Liberal Party. But we are fighting to achieve those things in which we believe, for which the party stands, and we must be prepared to do that in the most effective way possible.

There was pandemonium throughout. Bits had leaked overnight and at a given signal a hundred or so placards with the word 'no' were raised by delegates, mainly Young Liberals, standing shouting in their places. The rest of the audience counter-applauded and stamped while the press and TV cameras roamed madly. What was already a long speech looked like lasting an eternity.

I stood in disbelief looking at the seething hall for what seemed an hour but can't have been more than two or three minutes, and then continued to my well meant but in the circumstances poorly delivered peroration. The audience rose and cheered, perhaps I thought needing to stretch their cramped limbs, but even the critics mostly joined in. The assembly had backed the new line, but neither they nor I realized that the theory was going to be put to the test within six months.

Chapter 4

Towards Lib–Lab

When the 1976–7 session of parliament opened as usual in November the Commons found itself with three different party leaders from those who had assembled after the October 1974 general election. The mounting rates of inflation and unemployment inherited from the Tory government had continued unchecked by the Labour government. The government's majority had been whittled away by two vacancies, two defections and a series of Tory by-election victories and the opinion polls showed a continuing nationalist threat to Labour especially in Scotland. But the government embarked on a full session's programme including the intention to legislate for elected assemblies in Scotland and Wales.

On Armistice Sunday I assembled for the first time with others to lay wreaths on the Cenotaph. The order was clearly: Callaghan, Thatcher, Steel followed by ex-prime ministers, of whom only Ted Heath regularly turns up. In the interminable waiting in the corridors of the Home Office beforehand I therefore acted as an uncomfortable buffer between the Tory leader and her predecessor who did not appear to be on the chummiest of terms. I had arranged to have lunch with Ted Heath after the ceremonies. When he was Prime Minister I scarcely knew him and such little conversation as we had ever had consisted of stilted pleasantries. But since his demotion I had got to know him slightly in the European campaign and of course in the Commons his traditional seat is immediately in front of mine. Therefore I had exchanged words with him from time to time and expressed my approval of his increasingly wise and independent speeches on devolution, foreign affairs and the economy. 'Let's talk some time,' he had said, and so I suggested Sunday lunch that day since I was at a loose end having no real home base in London.

We left by separate routes in separate cars, and I arrived at his house in Wilton Street with its bomb-proof windows. I was nonetheless spotted by someone, presumably paid by the *Daily Mail* gossip column, who thought the event noteworthy. It is one of the more ridiculous features of our political system that MPs of different parties may chat in the Commons (though the members' dining room tables are segregated politically) but are regarded with acute suspicion if seen in each other's company across the party divides. I have regularly entertained visiting Labour, Tory and Nationalist MPs at my home in Scotland, but it always has to be hush-hush. I recall one particularly ludicrous occasion when I had been having a private lunch at Roy Jenkins's London house. We sped back to the Commons in the back of the Home Secretary's official Rover with its crack police driver and detective in the front. I was unceremoniously dumped at St James's Park lest we be seen driving together in through the gates of the Palace of Westminster. It is all utterly absurd and quite unlike political and social life in America or Europe.

Anyway, Ted Heath was very relaxed and welcoming. We lunched and talked mainly about politics and he surprised me by suddenly asking: 'Has Callaghan talked to you yet?' 'No,' I replied, 'why should he?' 'He will,' was the terse response. I had no reason to think any such thing would happen in the near future, though much later Ted reminded me of his forecast.

The government began the new session by unveiling their major piece of legislation, the Scotland and Wales Bill. Although they had taken note of some of the minor criticisms of their previous devolution white paper, the Bill contained a substantial number of flaws. Its first defect was that it combined two wholly different systems of devolution for two different countries in one Act. Not only was this in itself a clumsy and muddled piece of legislation, but it guaranteed joint opposition from the mutually reinforcing bands of Scottish and Welsh filibusters, led by Tam Dalyell and Leo Abse.

Despite all its flaws (which are discussed in Chapter 8) we decided as a party long committed to devolution that we should support the principle of the Bill in the second reading division. This we did and on 16 December the Bill was approved by 292 to 247. It then proceeded as a constitutional measure to be considered line by line in a committee of the whole House, where we felt there was every chance of securing improving amendments to it. But we were wrong. The committee stage was a dispiriting experience with repetitious second-reading arguments from the opponents, and late-night sittings wearing the House down. Most serious, the government appeared unwilling to accept any amendments at all, using the whips to drive the non-attending members (who had not listened to debates in which the government had clearly lost the argument) through the lobbies to get their way.

We were particularly incensed at their resistance to proportional representation for the proposed assemblies, since this had been recommended by the Royal Commission on the Constitution under Lord Kilbrandon. But the Labour Party decided it was against their interests.

After fourteen days of debate the government decided to introduce the guillotine, or timetable motion, to limit the time of debate on each section of the Bill and so ensure its safe passage. There was no question of consulting us about this, or its precise nature. We were simply informed.

Naturally the government were assuming that, despite their own dissidents, they could rely on the support of nationalists and Liberals (though not the few Tories) who had backed the second reading. I realized that our votes were crucial to their arithmetic and that we should use our muscle.

I persuaded the parliamentary party (strongly supported in the argument by Jo Grimond, but with our two Welsh colleagues dissenting) that we should oppose the guillotine and make our continuing support for the measure dependent on proper consultation and attention to Liberal views. Jo pointed out that if the guillotine were carried whole chunks of the Bill would go through without even the chance to debate Liberal amendments, never mind carry them. I decided to speak in the timetable debate myself.

Our threat was regarded with disbelief by the government who assumed we were bluffing, and dismay by sections of the Scottish and Welsh Liberal parties as well as vituperation from the nationalists, who could not understand how such a pro-devolution party could bring themselves to cause the legislation to grind to a halt. The guillotine failed to carry by twenty-nine votes. Our own opposition had encouraged further rebellion on the government side.

Thereafter the government announced that before proceeding further with the measure, they would hold talks with the other parties 'to seek the widest possible measure of agreement in parliament' on getting it going again. The Tories refused to participate on the ostensible grounds that they were against the Bill anyway, but in fact because they had an embarrassing lack of any agreed policy to bring to such discussions. The Scottish National Party (SNP) refused to participate because they thought the guillotine should have been a vote of confidence and considered the devolution Bill effectively dead. They would campaign for independence.

This left the Liberals talking constructively to the government about changes in the legislation which we had been unable to achieve in the House. It was a significant foretaste of the Lib–Lab pact itself, and the episode also demonstrated usefully to the government that Liberals meant what they said.

'I see now what you were after,' said a puzzled and critical Scottish Liberal to me in the anxious aftermath of the guillotine vote, 'you thought it necessary to kick them in the teeth before extending the hand of friendship.'

'Not quite the way I would have chosen to put it,' was my assenting reply.

Early in March with the International Monetary Fund (IMF) restraints as yet showing no signs of bringing about a reduction in inflation (the December–February annual rate running at over 20 per cent) and with the government's regular voting strength down to 310 out of the 631 voting Members of the House, Cyril Smith proposed that we should explore the possibility of securing some agreement with the government in return for our support. I was not over-keen on such a brazen approach but agreed that Cyril should do this off his own bat and entirely unofficially. He argued that he knew Callaghan from his days in the Labour Party and would be able to have a quiet word in his ear to sound him out. He wrote to the Prime Minister who was just about to leave for Washington who replied saying Cyril might like to talk instead to Cledwyn Hughes.

Cyril, who despite his bluff, rough, exterior, is one of the kindest and most sensitive souls in politics, took this as a rebuff and told me he had no intention of doing any such thing. I did not so interpret it since I knew Cledwyn could play a vital role, not just as Chairman of the Parliamentary Labour Party but as a lifelong friend and confidant of Jim Callaghan.

The following week the *Daily Mirror* carried a story about the Smith/Callaghan exchange, doubtless leaked by Cyril who was still very cross about it. According to Simon Hoggart of *The Guardian* Hughes and Callaghan discussed the public story and Callaghan was concerned lest the episode be seen as a snub to the Liberals. Therefore Hughes undertook to talk to me. At any rate, Cledwyn telephoned me to say no such snub was intended and I seized the opportunity to invite him round to my room for a chat.

This was on Thursday 17 March, the same day as the regular debate on public expenditure was taking place. Cuts in public spending of £2,500 million had been announced but the government, fearing revolt in their own ranks, refrained from putting this sum in a motion for debate and approval. Instead the debate was on the adjournment.

John Pardoe made it clear that in common with all the other parties we would vote against the government at the end of the day because the cuts were only necessary as a result of the incompetence of the government over the last three years. Cledwyn sought confirmation from me that this was so and told me that therefore the government were bound to lose. This would almost certainly be followed by a 'no confidence' debate which they might also lose. The Prime Minister wished me to understand that there would be an election.

I told Cledwyn that I understood this quickly snowballing crisis but that the Liberals had no cause to seek postponement of an election unless there were proper agreement and consultation between us on the future programme of the government. Cledwyn sent the Prime Minister a note of our meeting.

That night the government, knowing they would lose the adjournment vote, simply failed to put in either tellers or their troops through the lobby so that the motion to adjourn was carried unanimously. This was thought to be less humiliating than an actual two-or-three vote defeat, but the effect was the same. The government were on the run. But by avoiding a technical defeat they avoided the need to table their own immediate vote of confidence next day.

Instead the initiative passed to the official Opposition. The government had bought a few days' time, and after the vote Mrs Thatcher did not know quite what to do. Next (Friday) morning she called the shadow cabinet hurriedly together and they decided to table a vote of no confidence.

I had travelled by overnight sleeper back to Scotland and was conducting my weekly 'surgery' at my constituency office in Galashiels when Cledwyn Hughes came on the line to tell me of the Tory move. Just before it was announced, the Tory whips delivered a copy of their no confidence motion to our whip's office. At 11am Mrs Thatcher told the Commons of their intention and Michael Foot as Leader of the House said the debate would take place next Wednesday.

A Gallup poll in the previous day's *Daily Telegraph* had put the Tory lead over Labour at $16\frac{1}{2}$ per cent, enough for a Tory landslide if there were an election following a government defeat.

At twelve o'clock I issued a statement setting out how we would proceed as a party:

> I have called a meeting of the Liberal MPs for Tuesday morning to consider our position on the confidence motion. Our views have been made quite clear and public. Either the government now proceeds on the basis of agreed measures in the national interest for the next two years, in which case we would be willing to consider supporting such a programme, or else we have a general election in which the people can return a new House of Commons. The one thing we cannot do is stagger on like last night with a lame duck Labour programme which has neither public nor parliamentary support. The political decisions as to which course to take therefore rests squarely with the Prime Minister and the Labour Party.
>
> After the defeat on the devolution guillotine the government announced that they would proceed to seek 'the widest possible measure of agreement in parliament'. They must now say whether that principle is to apply to the whole of the government's programme.

In fact I fixed an earlier meeting of the Liberal MPs for late Monday night for an open-ended discussion without pressure from the press. Fortunately for the rest of Friday I was unobtainable, recording a Border Television programme in Carlisle in the afternoon, and travelling to Nelson, Lancashire, for the radio programme *Any Questions* in the evening. On both broadcasts I stuck to the line in my statement, and drove through the late night back to my home at Ettrick Bridge, thankful that not too many police patrols were travelling on the M6 as I kept the needle hovering between 90 and 100 mph.

On Saturday morning I issued a further statement designed to increase pressure on the Parliamentary Labour Party through the Sunday papers:

The confidence vote next Wednesday should wonderfully concentrate the minds of Labour MPs over this weekend and I hope they will convey their views to the party leadership. They must grasp that people in this country will not understand if they insist on committing suicide. They will do this if they refuse to compromise and seek a broader understanding in parliament.

It would be in the best interests of this country if it now begins to be governed on the basis of enjoying the widest public and parliamentary support for a programme of national recovery. If the Labour Party does not respond and acknowledge the political reality that it cannot continue to push on with full-blooded socialist government because there is no mandate for it, then the thirteen Liberal votes will be bound to be cast against the government in favour of a general election at which we would put our case for an end to the domination of parliament by any one extreme – Socialist or Thatcherite.

In the afternoon Bill Rodgers, the Minister of Transport, telephoned, having talked to the Prime Minister. This was the first approach via a member of the cabinet. Since we had worked together in the Europe campaign we could speak freely to each other. Bill undertook to convey my now rather more specific view concerning a possible agreement with the government to the Prime Minister, who was spending the weekend at Chequers.

On Saturday evening, in anything but a quiet and relaxed mood, I attended the production of *My Fair Lady* by the Selkirk Amateur Operatic Society in which our foster-son Billy had a medium-sized song and dance part. My mind could not have been further from the rain in Spain falling mainly in the plain.

Sunday was hectic. I had arranged to do a live interview at noon with the PM's son-in-law Peter Jay on London Weekend's prestige programme *Weekend World*. To the rage of producers who imagine they are bestowing an honour, I refuse to come running to their studios to the disruption of my family life. Against their will, they agreed to my doing it 'down the line' from Edinburgh with Peter Jay in London. This suited me fine since Judy and I were due for lunch at John Mackintosh's home in Edinburgh. John was of course very excited by what was happening and full of encouraging advice.

We sped back to Ettrick Bridge where I took calls from both Cledwyn Hughes and Bill Rodgers who said the Prime Minister wished to see me early on Monday evening. I accepted, and spent most of Sunday evening telephoning colleagues and my staff advising them how to handle the matter.

On Monday morning while I was on my way by train from Carlisle to Birmingham for the by-election at Stechford, my office was duly agreeing with the PM's office the announcement that 'The Prime Minister has invited Mr Steel to meet him in the Commons this evening.'

On my way to Carlisle near-disaster struck as I rushed for the train. In the Ettrick Valley I hit a pheasant which removed my front numberplate. I placed the offending bird in the boot for Judy to cook when she took the car home again, and as I sped through the outskirts of Carlisle I was stopped by a police patrol who couldn't decide whether to be more interested in my speed or lack of numberplate. When he recognized me the officer was charity itself. 'I know, you're rushing to see the Prime Minister.' It was, I thought, at least an original excuse.

The by-election campaign in Roy Jenkins's old seat was thrown into total confusion. I fluffed my way through a press conference and television interviews originally designed to be relevant to the by-election but now wholly transformed to the bemusement of our candidate and his agent. I then left by train for London with my personal assistant Andrew Gifford warding off the press, apart from an ITN interview I decided to give on the train itself to keep the pot boiling for the six o'clock news.

Meantime the Prime Minister's office were asking mine whether Michael Foot could attend the meeting at 6pm. They replied quite properly that no answer could be obtained until I arrived in London. At 5pm we arrived and with the help of police and station officials waded through the photographers to my car. En route to the Commons I considered the Foot question. I did not want to cause offence but I thought I should really have a first go over the ground with the Prime Minister alone.

We arrived at the Commons half an hour before the meeting and a message was sent using the excuse that I would have agreed to Foot's presence if I'd had time to get hold of John Pardoe, but since that was not possible I would rather not. At six o'clock prompt I walked the hundred yards of carpeted and wood-panelled corridors separating my office from the Prime Minister's room to begin our discussions.

My relations with James Callaghan were not at all close. He had patted me on the head as a new boy in 1965 a little more warmly than most on learning that as Labour's spokesman on the colonies under Attlee he had stayed a night at the home of my prospective in-laws in West Africa since they were about the only non-Tories to be found in that part of the world. That was the only connection we had.

Then in 1968 when he was Home Secretary I fell out with him fiercely over his Bill against the East African Asians. Although this was in no sense a personal quarrel, I felt strongly about it and was, as still a junior backbencher, no doubt rude to him. In 1971 he led for the opposition on the committee stage of the Tory Immigration Act, on which I was the Liberal representative. We joined forces in public on several amendments but there was little coming and going between us privately. Indeed he was fond of teasing me on my announcement in that committee (it included several all-night sittings which the bigger parties operated in relay teams) that it was Liberal policy to go home at midnight. (More recently he has pro-claimed that all decent people should be in bed by eleven, so perhaps even then there was a basic understanding between us!)

Just after that he was appointed shadow foreign secretary in one of Wilson's team reshuffles. We happened to share a taxi from the Commons to some lunch in London and I asked after his health following his prostate operation. I told him my father-in-law had just undergone the same thing and it knocked him out for about three months. He said he was indeed feeling frail and worried about whether he could cope physically with the role of shadow foreign secretary. Certainly at the time the press had foolishly written him off as an ageing has-been. In 1975–6 I overlapped as Liberal spokes-man on foreign affairs and I suppose I had at most two or three meetings with him as Foreign Secretary, mainly on Uganda and Rhodesia. On my becoming leader of the party in July 1976 he had formally congratulated me but we had never met for private discus-sion except once, with others, on the subject of devolution and I think once briefly on immigration.

That was our total experience of each other as I walked into his room with his principal private secretary, Ken Stowe. Even though it is only a staging post compared with the Downing Street office, the Prime Minister's room at the Commons is a spacious one in a suite of three, compared with the two 'railway carriage' type rooms

I have as leader of the Liberals. There is a large oval table round which ministers can sit if restricted to the House and he sat at one side motioning me to sit beside him. Ken Stowe sat opposite taking notes.

He began by repeating that a defeat on Wednesday would mean an election and I told him that was not a prime consideration for us. I said we were not interested in any covert arrangement to stave off defeat for Wednesday, but only in an open longer-term agreement which would involve consultation with us on the government's programme with particular emphasis on control of inflation through incomes policy, devolution and direct elections to Europe. The mood was sombre but amicable and we talked for over an hour, at the end of which he gave me sufficient encouragement to think that such an arrangement could be possible for me to put it to my colleagues that evening and him to discuss it with some of his.

Immediately after, at 7.15pm, I had a meeting in my room with the chairman and secretary-general of the Liberal Party, Geoff Tordoff and Hugh Jones. They brought the report I had asked them to compile by telephone region by region of how well the party was prepared for an election. Their conclusion was that though the party was not anxious for an election we were marginally more ready than in February 1974. The overwhelming view of the party was: 'if no concessions are forthcoming the MPs should vote against the government on Wednesday. Only if the concessions are cast-iron and public should we support the government.' Typical of the regional surveys was London where out of seventy-five constituencies where soundings were taken sixty-two favoured pushing the government to the limit and only thirteen expressed anxiety about an election.

It greatly strengthened the hand of the MPs and backed in comprehensive detail the public statement made by Tordoff the previous afternoon.

I have now completed the consultations which the leader of the Liberal Party asked me to undertake on Friday, having spoken to the chairmen of the national and regional parties in Scotland, Wales and England. I will be reporting to David Steel tomorrow that the rank and file of the party are solidly behind the line he and his colleagues are taking in relation to the vote of confidence on Wednesday.

While Liberals do not seek an early general election, and

believe a Thatcher government would be an unmitigated disaster, they believe Liberal MPs should vote against the government unless cast-iron assurances are given by the Prime Minister to David Steel that will lead to a genuine programme of national recovery.

If the government fails in its clear duty to govern from a broader basis of consent than it now enjoys, then it must go, and Liberals will face a general election with confidence in the knowledge that the Labour Party has brought about its own downfall.

The message from Liberals all over the country is 'bend or be broken'.

At eight o'clock I had dinner with John Pardoe in the members' dining room and briefed him on my meeting. At 9.45pm he went to see Michael Foot on a separate assignment organized by the unlikely go-between Eric Heffer, and at 10.45 we began our first and secret meeting of the parliamentary party in my overcrowded room. This lasted until midnight. It was agreed especially in the light of the report from the party that we would not do as badly in a general election as the commentators believed and we should feel no compulsion to come to an agreement, but the general outline of what I had suggested was agreed. My main argument was that we had tried realignment in opposition over nearly twenty years and it had not come off. Now was a chance to try it in government.

We arranged to meet, as publicly announced, the following day to consider whatever draft agreement I could obtain. I therefore started to commit my outline to paper. At eleven o'clock the Prime Minister's office was told that my proposals in draft were on their way and we agreed to meet at 12.30 to discuss them. My first draft consisted of six points.

I wrote to the Prime Minister as follows:

My colleagues have unanimously asked me to state that the Liberal Party will be prepared to consider sustaining the Government in its pursuit of national recovery on the following basis:

1) There would be set up a Consultative Committee between the two Parties, possibly under the chairmanship of the Leader of the House. Other membership to be discussed. To meet as required, but at least fortnightly during sittings

of the House. In addition to informal contacts of the kind already established between ministers and appropriate Liberal spokesmen, these would attend this Committee as and when the agenda so required. Any major departmental Bill, White Paper or policy statement under preparation could be referred for discussion to the Committee by either Minister or Liberal spokesman. Liberals may also introduce policy proposals. This arrangement to last until the end of the present Parliamentary session, when both Parties will consider whether the experiment has been sufficiently fruitful to continue, in which case the proposals for the Queen's Speech in the next session would be considered by the Committee.

2) There will be an immediate meeting between the Chancellor and the Liberal economic spokesman before making this agreement to confirm that there is sufficient identity of view on an economic strategy based on restraint of prices and incomes increases and reductions in the burden of taxation on personal incomes.

3) The Government will undertake to introduce and commend to the House a Bill for direct elections to the European Parliament based on a proportional system.

4) Progress will resume with legislation for devolution, taking account of Liberal proposals already submitted. In any future debate on proportional representation for the devolved assemblies, no government whip will be applied against it in either House.

5) The Government will not proceed with the Local Government Direct Labour Bill announced in the Queen's Speech nor with 'proposals to ensure that banking and insurance make a better contribution to the national economy' foreshadowed in the manifesto. No measures of nationalisation will be introduced.

6) The terms of any agreement between us to be published as a formal exchange of letters.

At 12.30 I had my second meeting in the Prime Minister's room, this time with Michael Foot and the Prime Minister's political adviser Tom McNally present by my agreement, as well as Ken Stowe. We went through the letter. For face-saving reasons they did not wish to cause trouble in their ranks by specifying those things they would *not* do in a written agreement. I could add these in my speeches with as much effect. I agreed that this was so. The only item of contention was number three on European elections. This did not surprise me since Michael Foot and a fair chunk of the Labour Party were opposed both to direct elections and proportional representation (PR), the mixture of the two being positively poisonous. They said they did not think the government would agree to this but would consider it and prepare a draft agreement based on my letter and our talk for our evening meeting.

I had a hasty discussion with most of my colleagues after lunch to keep them informed, and we awaited the document. It did not arrive until 4.15pm and I discussed it with John Pardoe. We both agreed that it was not in a form we could recommend to our colleagues for acceptance, so vague was the wording at several points. At five o'clock I returned it to Ken Stowe with suggested alterations. I was watching the 5.45pm TV news in the whip's office when I was called by the PM to come and see him to discuss the draft right away with Michael Foot.

This was our third meeting, which like the second lasted about half an hour. Our main disagreement was still on the European question on which the government draft had proposed:

> We agree that the nature and composition of the present Parliament make it appropriate in certain circumstances to settle some issues on a free vote. One such issue is the form of voting for the European Assembly; and another is proportional representation in the proposed Scottish and Welsh Assemblies. When these matters come before the House the Government will offer free votes on them. In reaching its conclusions on the matter of direct elections the Government will take fully into account the known preference of the Liberal Party for a proportional system.

This contained no commitment to actual legislation for direct elections at all, but I was unable to alter their views on this, though they were flexible on other matters.

At 6.45pm I put the draft agreement to a lengthy meeting with my colleagues. They made several changes, in none of which I saw difficulties, but we wanted something firmer on European elections.

At 9pm our suggested redraft was sent round and just after 9.30pm the PM and I began our fourth meeting, this time with

Michael Foot and John Pardoe present. We soon ran into trouble on the European paragraph, and I suggested we left it to see if we could agree all the other paragraphs. We did, which left the European one isolated as the sole source of disagreement. It looked as though we were going to fail and at around 10.20pm John Pardoe left to give his gloomy but accurate TV interview on the *Tonight* programme.

Meantime it seemed a pity that our failure to agree this one issue should vitiate the prospects of everything else and plunge us into an election. We talked round and round the subject, with my doodling stronger drafts, to be sent next door for instant typing. Eventually we came up with a revised paragraph which I said I was prepared to commend to my colleagues. It promised introduction of a Bill, a choice of election systems in the preceding white paper, and account to be taken of the Liberal Party's strong views on that matter. The Prime Minister had patiently explained that he could not promise that which he could not get the Parliamentary Labour Party to deliver.

I understood that and accepted an important addition – his private assurances that when the time came he would back PR himself. I agreed that we could proceed only on a basis of trust, and left at 11.05pm to have final consultations with my colleagues on the redraft. Two had gone to bed and had to be reached by phone.

Richard Wainwright (MP for Colne Valley) would not answer his phone and I had to send a secretary round after midnight to hammer on the door of his flat and make him telephone me. John Pardoe returned from the TV studios at 12.30am and agreed that the final draft, though not as good as we wanted, was an acceptable improvement.

All were prepared to accept the final draft except Jo Grimond and David Penhaligon (MP for Truro) who doubted the wisdom of the whole exercise internally but were prepared to go along with it for the unity of the party. At 12.45am I phoned some minor amendments to the duty clerk at Number Ten and left for my flat via a next-morning newspaper stand after 1am.

At 10 o'clock on the morning of Wednesday, 'no confidence' day, I checked that the minor alterations were acceptable and the draft was going to the cabinet. I suggested I called round to Number Ten to learn the outcome, but was told the PM would come to the House to see me after the cabinet. I discussed with Ken Stowe the

"Say hello to David, everyone!"

'Hello, David — just to let you know I've brushed my teeth
and washed behind my ears, and I'd like to go to bed now ...'

'Oh, I'll quite understand if you don't catch me – but are you sure
you want me to go through the bottom of your boat?'

timing of the publication and it was agreed it would be given out after the PM's speech in the debate.

At 1.25pm Stowe phoned to say the cabinet had been rough, but all was agreed. I later discovered that Messrs Benn, Orme, Booth and Millan had dissented from the agreement. The PM was too pushed for time now to come over and he was preparing his speech for the afternoon. I ordered some sandwiches and started on mine.

The whole operation had been conducted without leaks and, despite speculation because some meeting between us was known, the Tories were taken utterly by surprise. Mrs Thatcher made an opening speech described in the *Telegraph* as 'hovering uncertainly between disaster and tragedy and finally settling on catastrophe'.

The atmosphere was electric when the PM thereafter announced the agreement between us, and I followed his speech amid much clamour from the Tory benches. The vote of no confidence failed to carry by 298 votes to 322 and our difficult period of partnership had begun.

Chapter 5

First Phase of the Agreement, March–June 1977

The 'Lib–Lab agreement' as we decided to call it was thus announced on the early evening of Wednesday 23 March 1977 and was a major preoccupation of newspapers, radio and television programmes for the next few days. In addition to handling these, I had to work fast to put flesh on the bones, get the machinery established and reshuffle our own spokesmanships appropriately. I therefore cancelled a speech I was due to make at the annual Anglo–German Königswinter conference in Germany (which I hated doing because it is one of the most interesting and yet relaxed weekends in the political calendar) and spent the next four days in meetings and on the telephone to my colleagues.

On the Thursday I had the first of what were to prove many meetings with Michael Foot as Leader of the House, this time a lengthy one to discuss the Lib–Lab consultative machinery. I told him that it would be necessary to reinforce my small team by bringing in some Liberal peers. He understood my problem and cheerfully agreed to overlook his normal antagonism to such creatures. I said I thought it might be appropriate to discuss some of my proposed changes of spokesman with the appropriate minister in an amicable way to ensure there was no incompatibility of opposite numbers that could jeopardize the agreement. Michael agreed that this would be useful.

The official minute of that meeting concisely records our discussion of the composition of the consultative committee itself:

> 5. *Mr Steel* thought the existence of the agreement and the desire not to jeopardise it would help with internal Liberal discipline. On the operation of the consultative committee *Mr Steel* said he had no fixed views and wanted the whole thing to be as flexible as possible, with no vast fixed membership requiring a lot of time from busy people. *Mr Foot* agreed. *Mr*

Steel thought the hard core could be confined to Mr Foot, the two Chief Whips and one other Liberal (Any objection to Mr Pardoe? No) with other Ministers and spokesmen being brought in as necessary. He saw the committee 'more as a symbol than a working organisation' exercising 'oversight of how the thing is going, not trying to do the work itself'. The great bulk of consultations on particular subjects could be between Ministers and Liberal spokesmen, and need only be referred to the committee if they ran into difficulties. He imagined that Ministers would be supported by civil servants and he hoped there would be no objection if Liberal spokesmen were also accompanied by advisers – either full-time paid staff or outside advisers such as academics. *Mr Foot* indicated that this would be acceptable. *Mr Steel* thought the committee should probably meet about once a fortnight, but they could see how it went. *Mr Foot* agreed. He indicated that the Prime Minister might see presentational and other advantage in having three members of the Government team – possibly Mr Rees. *Mr Steel* said this would be acceptable, but Ministers should not be overburdened and all the core membership need not attend every time. On reflection he thought it might help with internal difficulties if the Liberal team could be increased to three (Any view between Mr Smith and Mr Hooson? *Mr Foot* had a preference for Wales.) Mr Steel said it might be helpful, too, if it was made clear that he and the Prime Minister could attend the committee if they wished. He did not imagine the Prime Minister would ever want to attend, but he might find it useful and as a spokesman he had to wear more than one hat.

6. On the committee procedure *Mr Steel* accepted that the Lord President's office would service the committee and produce an agreed record. He did not think it would normally be necessary for other officials or advisers to be present. He thought discussion in the committee should be confidential. What was said to the press could be agreed ad hoc; they would normally only be given the subjects that had been discussed, and not the content of the discussion.

7. *Mr Foot* said the Government and the PLP [Parliamentary Labour Party] had recently agreed on a revised internal consultative machinery with their own groups on a similar kind of basis in some ways to that now being discussed. This meant

that on many issues the PLP would be consulted before the Liberal Party. *Mr Steel* accepted that this would be necessary to the formulation of a Government view before the Liberals were consulted.

I then asked Michael Foot to go over the immediate issues likely to arise. Again the minute records accurately:

FINANCE BILL

The agreement already provided for meetings between the Chancellor and the Liberal economic spokesman.

PRICES

Mr Steel said the question of prices legislation had made him aware of some of the transitional problems likely to be thrown up by policy issues already in the pipeline on which they would be asked if they had been consulted. In fact they had been consulted on prices before the present agreement, but had not responded. They would now say that they had been consulted and agreed with the principle of the Bill. This was not a blanket undertaking to support every clause or line, but he hoped there could be discussion with the Secretary of State before they pressed any disagreement to a vote.

For the future, he hoped they could see draft legislation and discuss possible Liberal objections before there was a confrontation on the Floor of the House. It might often be sufficient to agree the principle in advance without being tied to every jot and tittle.

POST OFFICE (AMENDMENT) – Industrial democracy

There had been some approach already *Mr Steel* thought, and some Liberal objection, although he had not been involved himself. They had also received a direct approach from the POEU [Post Office Engineering Union]. He thought this was an obvious case for immediate reference to the committee, where it could be discussed with the relevant Minister and Liberal spokesman present. *Mr Foot* said he thought there was a decent, reputable case for the Bill and they would try to persuade the Liberals of that. He agreed there should be a full-scale meeting next week.

OCCUPATIONAL PENSIONS

This was a longer, more elaborate Bill and *Mr Foot* did not regard it as so urgent. The Cabinet had not yet decided whether parliamentary time could be found for the Bill, although they were strongly in favour on the merits of the case. *Mr Steel* said they had strong reservations about this Bill and were keener on the principle of the Post Office Bill. If the Government wanted to go ahead on occupational pensions there should be consultations between spokesmen before there was any consideration of the matter by the committee.

SHIPBUILDING REDUNDANCIES

The Government were still consulting and *Mr Foot* could not say how or when they would wish to consult the Liberals. *Mr Steel* thought this was a Bill for discussion between Minister and spokesman.

OFFICE DEVELOPMENT PERMITS

Mr Steel thought the Liberals would support some renewal of the existing system. Again a case for discussion between Minister and spokesman.

LOCAL AUTHORITIES (WORKS)

Given the agreement that had already been reached *Mr Steel* did not think further discussion would be necessary – if it was their spokesman would be Mr Stephen Ross. He accepted that the Bill would include provisions to tighten up accounting as well as the renewal of existing powers.

9. On other matters that were coming before the House *Mr Steel* said his main aim was to ensure that Liberal spokesmen were well enough informed to be able to refer things to the committee if they seemed likely to be contentious enough to put the agreement in jeopardy. Decisions would have to be taken ad hoc on what was done about White Papers etc. It would be most helpful if they could have longer notice on statements where these were long planned rather than arose as a matter of urgency. What the Liberals said would be more closely scrutinized in future; where statements were repeated in both Houses he would like to achieve better co-ordination of the Liberal reaction.

10. *Mr Foot* and *Mr Steel* had a long discussion on devolution which is recorded separately for wider circulation. They agreed that there should be another meeting on devolution strategy next week, preferably on Monday afternoon. Mr Smith and the new Liberal spokesman (probably Mr Johnston) would attend and *Mr Foot* thought it important that he and *Mr Steel* should attend. There could be separate discussions about the Liberals' devolution memorandum.

11. *Mr Steel* thought the Liberals could abstain on the defence motion on Monday. If there seemed likely to be any difficulty the Chief Whips could consult.

12. *Mr Foot* said that a note on the committee and consultative procedures generally was being prepared for the Prime Minister and would be shown to Mr Steel.

13. The Lord President's office would tell the press that *Mr Foot* and *Mr Steel* had had a further very satisfactory exploratory meeting and had reached broad agreement on the composition of the consultative committee and the subjects to be discussed.

My reference on the topic of prices to 'transitional problems' was a wild understatement of what was to follow. For Tuesday 29 March was budget day, and of course the budget had been finalized before our agreement had been reached, and so naturally we had not been consulted on its contents. Therefore to our mutual horror the Lib–Lab ship struck a rock within a week of being launched when Denis Healey announced a $5\frac{1}{2}$ pence increase in fuel tax as well as increases in vehicle excise duties.

We were horrified because of course our Liberal constituencies would be those most hard hit by increases in the cost of transport. Moreover petrol already cost substantially more in these areas than in the cities. While we could not oppose increases in petrol tax for ever, especially since we were a conservationist party, we had the previous year drawn attention to these high prices in rural areas and demanded attention to them without success. We could scarcely therefore this year vote to make the situation even worse in our own seats in the name of our new political agreement which was in any case already under sustained attack by the Conservative Party.

We did the only thing possible: made it clear that the budget was not part of the agreement and that therefore we would be voting against these increases. The government were alarmed, and the day after budget day coincided with the first meeting of the Lib–Lab committee. Michael Foot was in the chair with Merlyn Rees as Home Secretary and his shadow Emlyn Hooson. John Pardoe led for us and the two chief whips, Michael Cocks and Alan Beith, completed the meeting with Sir Freddie Warren (the government whips' operator) in attendance.

After further discussion and agreement on the committee's own procedure (it would meet fortnightly on Wednesdays with the agenda agreed between the head of my office and the Lord President's private secretary) John Pardoe informed the meeting of our views on the petrol question (see Appendix 1).

On Monday after questions I saw the Prime Minister in his room where he reiterated what Joel Barnett had told John Pardoe at their Thursday meeting, namely that while sympathetic to our difficulty and accepting that this was unforeseen on both sides, no government could lose its budget resolutions and stay in office. He asked for our support at the end of the budget debate with continuing discussion on what to do about our own just-conceived agreement. We therefore faced the embarrassment of abstaining on the resolutions raising these taxes while sticking by our determination to do something about it next month in the Finance Bill.

The Lib–Lab ship sailed on with that nasty hole in its side for the next few weeks.

In the discussions which followed, it became painfully obvious that ministers who ought to have been consulted (e.g. Roy Hattersley at Prices and Bill Rodgers at Transport) simply bowed to Treasury diktat and had no foreknowledge beyond the cabinet briefing on such a matter affecting their departments. Indeed on the whole question of rural transport, David Penhaligon seemed to be conducting regular tutorials with Bill Rodgers whose Stockton-on-Tees constituency provides no background experience of the subject.

After a great deal of haggling, the government eventually dropped the $5\frac{1}{2}$ pence tax increase from petrol in the committee stage of the Finance Bill on 9 May. In return for our acquiescence on the similar derv increase in the budget, no compensating tax increase was sought for the £140 million thereby lost. The reduction took place on 5 August and was the first fruit of the Lib–Lab agreement to benefit the pocket of the man in the street.

The second meeting of the Lib–Lab committee took place the

day before we escaped thankfully into the calm of the Easter recess. The Tories had hounded the government constantly as to what was going on in the committee. Early on the Prime Minister and I had agreed that nothing would be said about it, under the 'no ministerial responsibility' rule. This meeting was a constructive discussion on the new Bill establishing industrial democracy in the Post Office. The Secretary of State for Industry, Eric Varley, and his Minister of State, Gerald Kaufman, joined the committee together with our industry spokesman Richard Wainwright. Wainwright had already had direct discussions with the unions and post office and the ministers and we were unhappy about a new board which was simply a management/union carve-up. We wanted specific consumer representation on the new board. It was agreed to delay publication of the Bill and to continue discussion after the recess.

At the resumed meeting on 20 April, Cyril Smith as our employment spokesman also joined the committee. What was proposed was a two-year experiment in industrial democracy on the board, but we wanted two consumer representatives in addition to the four independents proposed. During discussion, the government shifted from the proposed six government, six union, four independent formula to seven government, seven union and five independent, one to be specifically representing consumer interest. The Liberals declined to accept this, and subsequently the government agreed without a further meeting to two consumer representatives on the controlling body of this public monopoly in return for our support for the Bill. The two-year experiment was ended by the new Conservative government who were never enthusiastic. The system of union appointment proved less than successful.

Meantime the potentially explosive topic of direct elections was threatening to undermine the calm working of the agreement. At a meeting with the Prime Minister on 3 May we simply noted our continuing disagreement on the topic of petrol tax but were much more concerned about our agreement coming adrift over these elections. Our agreement had committed the government to stop shilly-shallying and actually introduce a Bill for direct elections, thus for the first time committing themselves fully to the process. But Callaghan was having difficulty getting the proposed proportional representation regional list system through the cabinet ('I got very angry,' he assured me) and even more difficulty with the Parliamentary Labour Party. I stressed that there was absolutely no hope of delivering a new agreement for next session, as we both wanted, unless he was able to persuade his colleagues to make the system their recommendation. I knew he was in deep trouble on this topic, but so was I, and we were therefore quite blunt with each other in facing the fact.

By this time I had started to record impressions in my diary for my own benefit, since so many meetings were taking place outside the Lib–Lab formal framework.

On 9 May I wrote:

> Roy Jenkins's wife rang over the weekend asking if I could lunch with him today, so I catch an early plane and join him at Wilton's (ludicrously expensive but with his salary at £60,000 not surprising). Apart from general chit-chat, his object is to tell me how much he relies on us keeping pressure on the government on direct elections.
>
> Evening dinner of European Movement at the Reform Club at which Roy makes a good speech. Lord Chalfont sitting near me makes noises about wanting to be a European candidate, possibly as a Liberal. He's been in and out before and some of his views are not Liberal.

We had a treble problem: 1. pressing the government to present the Bill in line with our European interest; 2. getting a recommendation for a PR system in the interests of preserving our agreement; 3. and not pressing on too quickly to make traditional first-past-the-post an easily available alternative with plenty of time for boundary commissions to draw up the eighty-one constituencies and hear objections.

On Wednesday 11 May I had lunch with Gaston Thorn, the Luxembourg Prime Minister and chairman of the European Liberals and Democrats, together with the Canadian Liberal Prime Minister, Pierre Trudeau, in a private room at the Reform Club. I solicited Gaston's help in keeping the British government to the May/June legislative deadline and discussed the threat of Quebec separation with Trudeau, who reckoned he would have to stay on as PM to stave it off. This was what finally caused his wife Margaret to depart because they had been hoping to return to a normal life. I felt strong sympathy for him.

On 24 May I was at Holyrood Palace, Edinburgh, for the Queen's Jubilee Banquet. The Prime Minister was also there, and by this time I had realized that the slow pace on producing the direct elections Bill was because of three threatened resignations from the cabinet. I arranged to travel back the next morning in his private plane in order to talk.

I noted the outcome of our journey in my diary next day:

> Stayed with Mother and Dad overnight. He drives me to Turnhouse. Executive jet waiting at RAF station, JC arrives and we get straight aboard with Audrey, Ken Stowe, detective and secretary. An hour to Northolt and lots of coffee and newspapers.
>
> JC spells out what his little meeting of ministers had concocted the day before on direct elections. The regional list will be in the Bill's main clauses, with a first-past-the-post schedule attached in case it is defeated. Sounds a strange device but acceptable. He is putting this to cabinet next day and hopes to get agreement. Asks me therefore not to let this information go further.

He also asked me about my views on attending official junkets. I had told Ken Stowe that I wanted to farm these out among my colleagues when appropriate as I found them excessively time-consuming, but I had encountered difficulty with one pompous official at the Palace. 'Leave it to me', Stowe had said and there on the plane was the first fruit of his work: 'Did I want to dine at Number Ten with the Commonwealth prime ministers as well as at Buckingham Palace?' I politely declined and they agreed to ask Jeremy and Marion Thorpe instead, since he was Foreign and Commonwealth spokesman.

I had already been teased by Prince Charles at Buckingham Palace for turning up wifeless, because Judy was necessarily looking after our young family at home and we agreed she could not trail south for every important function.

She did, however, abandon them for the Jubilee Day celebrations on 7 June, only to find me slipping quietly off to Number Ten in the afternoon. I recorded that strange day as follows:

> Jubilee Day
> Tuesday 7 June 1977
> J and I travelled overnight by sleeper from Berwick. Supposed to be met by BBC car at Kings Cross but it didn't turn up.

Went to Broadcasting House by taxi and off-loaded luggage in reception area which J sat and looked after while I went to studio for early morning radio interview on Lib–Lab agreement.

Then to our flat for quick bath. Hired car and driver took us to St Paul's. Sat next to the Thatchers. After the magnificent service came out by the wrong door following various ministers, who turned out not to be going to the Guildhall. Therefore missed the special coaches and had to walk through the crowded streets – all very jolly but a bit embarrassing with me in full kilt regalia.

Bumped into PM on going into the Guildhall and we agreed to meet at Number Ten at 5.15 (I had phoned Ken Stowe over the weekend and suggested a meeting to clarify procedure on direct elections). Total confusion again on leaving Guildhall because there was no system for calling up the cars. Found Ted Heath equally lost. Eventually both shepherded out side entrance, where car was drawn up. A good cheer from the crowd and I did a lot of hand shaking en route to the car. People are either in very festive mood or the Liberal Party is more popular than I thought.

Half-hour doze then off to Downing Street. Arrived as requested by PM via Cabinet Office in Whitehall to avoid crowds. Staff member waiting and took me through connecting locked door to Number Ten. JC coming downstairs with Indian Prime Minister Morarji Desai, David Owen in tow. Stops to introduce me and we indulge in some light-hearted banter with Desai's encouragement before they move out to the main door where they get a cheer from a sizeable crowd.

Upstairs to a drawing room. JC mutters 'Desai takes ages to come to the point.' I said: 'Well I won't – party very ruffled by press reports on government handling of direct elections and I seek clarification and reassurance.'

JC repeats formula he told me in the plane. PR in the Bill, with first-past-the-post option in schedule. He has to have a free vote on the Bill to avoid resignations but doesn't like it. Faces PLP Thursday 16th, Bill to be published following week. Debate early July and second reading, thereafter committee.

I press him on whether PR will be government recommendation. He says at first no – free choice for House. I stress impor-

tance of interpreting main body of the Bill as being the government recommendation which Rees will commend. He takes the
point, and says of course he will vote for it himself.

I caution against proceeding as far as a vote on the system
of election before summer recess because we could lose; and
that would endanger the agreement because the party, especially at conference, would get very upset. He says Bill could
probably be redrafted or retimed to avoid this. I point out that
by autumn the case for PR on time grounds is greatly strengthened. He accepts this.

He also believes guillotine will be necessary in the autumn
– 'presumably on a free vote also?' I ask – 'Yes'.

In other words we are going to have to screw up the Tories
to get this through. We leave on the agreed note that we haven't
a clue what they might do, but I remain optimistic that it can
be done. We must lobby Labour first and then Tories.

As I leave JC mentions good export figures to be published
next week. I don't know whether this is intended to keep himself or me cheerful.

Our next meeting was on 13 June. I had always made it my policy
not to seek unnecessary meetings. The Prime Minister's life was
hell enough without having the leader of the Liberal Party darting
in and out every other day. On average we met therefore perhaps
once a fortnight. He had had a particularly hectic time and the direct
elections issue was clearly a nagging nuisance as my note of that
day shows:

Monday 13 June 1977

The House returned after the Whitsun recess. I am met off
the plane at Gatwick with a request to appear on ITN's lunchtime news on the subject of direct elections. The morning's
press full of gloom on this issue.

After the broadcast, lunch with Jeremy Thorpe in the Commons when I fill him in on my discussions so far with the PM.
We agree that I should write to PM expressing concern about
free vote plus schedule proposal.

I cancelled dinner with Indian PM, because of amount of
work, expecially speech to American Chamber of Commerce
next day. Arranged to dine with Alan Beith at 8pm in the
members' dining room. Just got there when telephone call from

Ken Stowe asked me to see PM in a few minutes when he was finished with the Chancellor.

8.15 I meet JC in his room. He has draft of the Bill in his hands and outlines provisions. Part II to be PR regional list. Part III as option for first past the post. He objects to my strictures on the free vote saying it is a matter for him. I agree but say he should know our reaction. Putting both systems in the body of the Bill was not 'better' as he described but 'worse' in our eyes.

I ask for a government recommendation. He says rather huffily that he hasn't had a cabinet since we last spoke and he's been busy with the Commonwealth conference.

We leave on rather cool terms for the first time. I return rather angrily to the dining room and tell AB and JT of unsatisfactory meeting. I urge JT to see Rees next day.

My colleagues became justifiably restive and fortunately active on the issue as my next two days' entries show:

Tuesday 14 June 1977

JT sees Rees and expresses alarm about inclusion of both methods in the Bill. He phones David Owen to say the same and sees Cledwyn Hughes as chairman of PLP before PLP meeting tonight. I see Bill Rodgers to stiffen him and make it clear that unless the cabinet on Thursday is more decisive there will be no new agreement next session. Chat to John Mackintosh before the meeting as well.

Met Cledwyn Hughes afterwards who says PLP meeting went not badly and suggests I keep up pressure on cabinet members before Thursday and if possible see PM again.

Wednesday 15 June 1977

JT sees Harold Lever. Frank Byers sees Fred Peart and Elwyn-Jones. I see Shirley Williams.

Party meeting at 6pm agrees to take firm line on PR for direct elections without any dissent. 7.15pm JT, JP and AB meet in consultative committee with Michael Foot and Merlyn Rees, and we await cabinet decision tomorrow. They were still not shown text of the Bill.

The meeting of the consultative committee on 15 June was devoted wholly to the direct elections Bill, which they were not shown. Jeremy Thorpe joined our side for the meeting. He, John Pardoe and Alan Beith presented our views firmly as the minute makes clear:

DIRECT ELECTIONS

Mr Foot said that the date of introduction of the Direct Elections Bill would be announced on Thursday. The plan was to publish the Bill on 23 June and for Second Reading to take place in early July. The Bill would not be enacted this Session and it would be reintroduced at the beginning of next. Discussions about the form of the Bill had taken place between the Prime Minister and Mr Steel and between Mr Rees and Mr Thorpe. The matter had been carefully considered and the Bill had been so drafted that the regional list (RL) system would apply unless the House by resolution substituted first past the post (FPP). *Mr Steel* had expressed the hope that there would not be a vote on the method of election in the present Session. Accordingly the order of the clauses had been arranged so that, even if the Bill went into Committee, the point would not be reached where there could be a vote on the electoral method. *Mr Foot* said they believed that the form of the Bill offered the best prospect of success for a RL system.

Mr Thorpe said that in the context of their agreement the Government had changed its ground on direct elections by the decision to have a free vote on the principle as well as on the method of election. The Liberals would forbear on this but he was not clear what the Government would achieve by including FPP in the Bill when the House was being given a free vote. He asked why the Home Secretary did not simply introduce a Bill containing RL and he queried whether both systems had the same standing in the Bill.

Mr Rees said that a FPP system could not be introduced in 1978 because there was now insufficient time for the Boundary Commission to complete its work. *Mr Thorpe* commented that if this were made clear – and questions in debate might make it necessary for the Home Secretary to do so – it could have a beneficial effect in attracting support for RL from some pro-marketeers who might otherwise incline towards FPP.

Mr Thorpe said that there was no suggestion that the Government were seeking to outmanoeuvre the Liberals. He understood the points which Mr Foot had made and why in the circumstances that a Bill could not be enacted this Session, it was thought best to proceed in the way proposed. But in the context of renegotiating the agreement, the Liberal position in both the House and the country was that Europe represented the only subject on which they could act and on which Liberals could judge the worthwhileness of the agreement – it was unlikely that Phase III and devolution matters would be sufficiently advanced for such judgements to be made in time to influence renegotiation. If the Bill remained in its present form it would be essential to make clear what the Government view was; and unless there was a recommendation for RL the Liberals would see no point in the agreement. Whilst it was not meant as a threat the fact was that a clear recommendation was the minimum necessary to enable the Liberals to renegotiate. *Mr Pardoe* commented that in terms of the number of members in Europe which each Party would achieve there were clear advantages in the Labour Party – as well as the Liberals – supporting a regional list system.

There was some discussion about whether the Government should indicate what its recommendation would be, and the reasons for it, at the time the Bill was published. *Mr Thorpe* – strongly supported by Mr Pardoe and Mr Beith – said that it was essential that this be done (e.g. by a statement or a press release). The Bill was unusual in that it included a choice of systems and a lot of steam could be taken out of any criticism if the Government explained its approach when the Bill was published. *Mr Pardoe* commented that unless the Government's approach was explained at the outset, 'ribaldry would kill the Bill before Second Reading was reached'.

Mr Foot said that the Cabinet had not yet considered the choice of electoral systems. Their instruction had been to prepare the way for direct elections in a sensible manner which satisfied the obligations to the Liberals. This had been done but the Cabinet had not yet considered the Bill. What the Liberals were now seeking went beyond the terms of the agreement (and Mr Foot read out the relevant part). *Mr Thorpe* accepted that this was the case and that what had been proposed by the Government was fully in accord with the agreement. However, what the Liberals were now saying, in their view, was within the spirit of the agreement and did not go beyond what Liberals in the country thought it meant.

Mr Foot said he would put the points which the Liberals had made to the Cabinet. He hoped that it would be possible to agree to proceed on the basis that the Bill remained unchanged. The points made by the Liberals would be taken fully into account in deciding how to proceed and if necessary he would arrange a further discussion following the Cabinet considerations.

The next day the argument continued before and after the cabinet as my diary noted:

Thursday 16 June 1977

Telephone Merlyn Rees before the cabinet meeting to stress objection to present form of direct elections Bill.

After the meeting Foot asks to see me and tells me cabinet has deferred decision for another week. I repeat request for 'Part III' to be demoted to schedule and the government to give clear recommendation on PR. Also need for government to get its troops into line on devolution before the recess. He says this will be difficult.

Michael Foot and David Owen drop in separately in the early evening to assure me that all is going well inside the cabinet on the European front.

The argument continued in two further meetings on 20 and 21 June, one with myself and Michael Foot and at the second joined by Merlyn Rees and Jeremy Thorpe and a parliamentary draughtsman. We went over the whole ground again, at the end of which both Foot and Rees promised to press our demand to downgrade the FPP option and for the government to make a clear recommendation on the PR system in the form of the Bill.

I was determined to revert to the proposal the Prime Minister had made on our private plane journey and which I thought the minimum we could accept. The cabinet eventually agreed; the Bill was reprinted in that form and published on 26 June with the government explaining its recommendation for the regional list system.

On 5 July, two days before the second reading debate, I went to see the Speaker to confirm that, as already advised by the clerks, he would not call the cunning 'reasoned amendment' on second reading which if carried would have excluded the regional list system. He took the point, naturally without giving a commitment. In the event that reasoned amendment was not selected and the Bill safely received its second reading on 7 July.

Thereafter it was quietly dropped amid unsuccessful Tory agitation that a decision should be taken on FPP to enable the Boundary Commission to press ahead. Merlyn Rees successfully stalled this.

But the direct elections issue was to prove a slow fuse which would smoulder through to the autumn threatening to blow up the agreement. I knew it because of the original difficulty on this point in drafting the agreement. The government knew it, or at least Messrs Callaghan and Foot did, and the Tories suspected it.

Chapter 6

The Agreement is Renewed

By mid-June the pact had been in operation for three months and with no sign of any revival of Liberal fortunes in the opinion polls or at local government by-elections there was already a fair amount of pressure building up in the Liberal Party to let the thing die at the end of the session, i.e. in October, though effectively in July, since there was unlikely to be much of a carry-over of the old session after the summer recess. At the same time the government were going to want to know towards the end of July whether we were going on with them into a new session, or whether they faced the bleak options of a return to day-to-day minority government, or an autumn general election.

We agreed therefore to fix a two-day meeting of the shadow administration for Sunday and Monday 26-7 June to assess our own position and formulate a basis for renegotiating the pact for the next session if that were our decision. On 14 June, however, a new and disturbing factor came into that assessment. I noted that day:

> John Pardoe tells me that the government has been defeated several times in the Finance Bill Committee because Tribunites joined with the Tories on tax cuts while he was left supporting the government. The Labour Party does seem to be more of a disorganized rabble than the Liberal Party. We discuss whether it is possible to keep them going on this basis.

The next morning I was recording a television party political broadcast. I was rather put out by what John had told me, because there was little point in our supporting the government in their unpopular decisions to enable them to obtain such crucial legislation as their Finance Bill if their own supporters felt free to do as they pleased on attractive populist amendments tabled by the Tories. What made their action more annoying was that we too would have liked to back the concessions but had to support the agreed budget balance.

I decided therefore to add a section to my script warning the Labour Party of the possibility of non-renewal of the agreement because of their disunity and reluctance to back the Prime Minister on his policies.

> I am not sure whether we will be able to secure another agreement, because especially after yesterday the Labour Party is proving a difficult, fragile and internally divided partner. Unless they pull themselves together we may have to have an election in the autumn. But I am sure we are right to try this new experiment in political co-operation. For the first time since the last war politicians are sinking their differences to try to solve the country's problems. We may not succeed but surely it is worth trying.

I did an interview on the radio programme *The World at One* on the same theme and gave a lobby press briefing using advance text of the TV broadcast that afternoon.

On Friday I was to address the annual conference of the Scottish Liberal Party at Aviemore. I added a passage to my speech directed to next Tuesday's meeting of the Parliamentary Labour Party emphasizing the pointlessness of our reaching agreement with the government on policies if their own supporters would not deliver the votes. The rest of the speech was mainly an outline of our terms for supporting a new devolution package. The speech was well reported by the exceptionally large press and broadcasting corps attending the conference.

Next morning there was a typical episode of media panic. I was supposed to be attending the morning sessions of the conference, but over breakfast both Archy Kirkwood and David Miller of the Scottish Liberal Party alternately brought me fresh rumours of a public announcement due at 11am from Number Ten. The press thought it could be an election announcement or even the Prime Minister's resignation.

A kind of fever grips all reporters on such occasions. They all wanted to line up interviews immediately after and preferably before the announcement. Instead of going to the conference hall therefore I dispatched Graeme, who had travelled with me for the weekend, with some money to sample the delights of the leisure centre while I stayed in my hotel room ready to receive any official word of what was in store and the stream of press rumours. As I

expected, the Prime Minister simply issued a weekend homily calling on the Labour Party to stick together, taking a swipe at the
Tories and announcing his determination that the government
would carry on. I gave suitably muted and matter-of-fact comment
afterwards. Several Sunday papers carried comments on how
Labour would have to come into line.

In the afternoon the conference formally debated 'the agreement'
as we were still careful to call it. So overwhelming was the endorsement of it that we had to prod a leading Scottish Liberal into voicing
his inner reservations against it since otherwise there would have
been a colourless and unreportable debate. The Scottish party was
much more enthusiastic about it than the English party, mainly
because of the extra dimension of the devolution talks.

On the following Tuesday the Parliamentary Labour Party
appeared suitably sobered and that evening we spent all night supporting the government in endless divisions on the prices Bill, our
continuous presence clearly making a favourable impact on the
Labour whips and their troops.

Next weekend came our two-day meeting at St Ermin's Hotel,
Westminster. Cyril Smith had been difficult before the meeting but
came round a bit during it. Jo Grimond and David Penhaligon, who
had been and still were opposed to the agreement, nevertheless felt
we now had to press on with tougher terms; the rest were sufficiently
agreed for us to be able to draw up a ten-point plan for the renegotiation with even the dissenters assisting in its compilation. We met
round a large green baize table and I went round everyone in turn
asking their views.

Russell Johnston argued that the devolution package was coming
along nicely. David Penhaligon said that did not matter in England
and a tough pay policy was more critical. Richard Wainwright said
the agreement needed more time to be seen to work and that we
should not precipitate an election by being too tough in backroom
negotiation. Michael Winstanley argued that everything hinged on
getting an advance on the electoral reform front. Eric Avebury was
in favour of renewal for one session at a time. Stephen Ross declared
he was in politics to change things and we should press on for as
long as possible, pulling out only if Phase III of the pay policy were
weak.

Jeremy Thorpe argued that we must be able to go into an election
showing we'd achieved something. Therefore we should abandon

the agreement only if the government proved downright impossible. Desmond Banks admitted that the danger of lost votes had been inevitable and wanted us to have more say in future in what was going to happen rather than reacting to events. Frank Byers felt we had not yet won enough. He was in favour of going right through to autumn 1979 if, say, we could get a referendum on proportional representation. Basil Wigoder was even more strongly in favour of going on, seeking an electoral pact if necessary. An election now would simply mean a Tory government. Nancy Seear had been talking to Ralf Dahrendorf (Director of the London School of Economics and former Liberal minister in his native West Germany) on his experience in the Free Democratic Party coalition with the SPD in Germany: we could only pull out on a real Liberal issue, and we should urge a strong government/TUC agreement on pay.

John Pardoe was in favour of a strategy to realign the parties and there was a chance to do this inside rather than outside government. The economy was the key. He was optimistic about 1978-9 and if we could help the government through this difficult patch we might enable a realigned left government to guide Britain through the prosperous 1980s. The Tories had failed to restructure industry in the prosperous 1950s. Tax reform should be a priority. George Mackie considered John's view of the economic future to be too rosy, but agreed with Russell on devolution. The unity of the parliamentary party was also vital and it was now much better. Emlyn Hooson cheerfully advanced the argument that we had been on a hiding to nothing before the agreement and the only difference now was that we were set on an even greater hiding to nothing, but we had 'got on' in Jo's phrase and must now show we were not scared of the heat. It had taken three months to sell the agreement to the party in Wales. It would therefore take longer to persuade the electorate. Cyril Smith disagreed with all that had been said so far. Circumstances had changed since the original agreement which he had supported. Phase III would fail. The left had increasing sway in the Labour Party. We had had a bad press because they wanted a Thatcher government. He believed it fatal if we went into the next election tied to the coat-tails of the Labour government. What reason would anyone have for voting for him in Rochdale? Thirteen, he now realized, was too small a number to manage such an agreement.

Jo Grimond said the press was not as bad as Cyril made out and we should take no decision to break the agreement now. We might have done quite well in a March election but we were now stuck with the course we had adopted. Economic issues were more important than direct elections or devolution. This was a bad old government and it was not going to get better.

Geraint Howells said the agreement had gone down badly at first in Wales but was now more popular. Reduction in petrol tax and raising VAT threshold were good examples of what had been done. More could be got out of a new agreement, especially on the self-employed and small business front. Geoff Tordoff, as party chairman, said there was wide support in the party for continuing the agreement. In particular there was appreciation of the MPs acting together and such unity was vital.

I summed up the discussion pointing out that we should only come out of the agreement if we could blame Labour for its failure, showing the Labour Party to be an impossible instrument, not because of failure of nerve on our part. Otherwise we go on. There was great stress on electoral reform in the party. Both the direct elections Bill and the devolution Bills would give us a chance to promote the cause further. Devolution was more important to the English members than they realized. If we failed to obtain it there could be an invasion of Nationalists at the next election risking our demotion to fourth party in the House. Electorally, the economy was the key issue and we must press for tax reform and profit-sharing in the next year. The party assembly in Brighton in September should be used to sell the agreement.

Discussion then continued and it was agreed that the negotiations on a new agreement should be completed before the party conference so that the government was forced to defend their side of it at their own conference. It was agreed that we should draw up a ten-point plan to put publicly to Labour. I made the proviso that this should only contain matters which the government were capable of delivering.

The meeting was in favour of renegotiation, not instant renewal, and with one or two reservations we accepted the alternative of an election in autumn.

(Clement Freud arrived fresh from the by-election at Saffron Walden with gloomy news of a Tory poll putting us a poor third. We all agreed that this by-election would be, whether we liked it or not, a crucial test of the electoral acceptability of the agreement.)

On Monday morning we digested the reports of the Prime Minister's weekend at Chequers with his cabinet, which by pure coincidence (which the press did not wholly believe) happened at the same time. I pointed out that the cabinet appeared to have recommitted itself to a further period of Lib–Labbery and this gave us more potential leverage.

John Pardoe then stressed Healey's optimistic assessments of the economy. He favoured backing a pay policy that would keep the earnings rise down to around 15 per cent without getting caught on specific figures. He wanted us to go hard for income tax cuts and outlined again the tax reform proposals of the economics panel. I argued strongly for profit-sharing. Cyril agreed but said any such schemes should fall outside pay policy. We spent Monday morning constructing our 'shopping list'. I summed up by pointing out that we now had noted forty-six suggestions and I proposed we should compress these to a manageable ten and this we did.

Most of the press next day led their front pages with our proposals. The *Daily Express* dubbed them the 'Ten Commandments' with the grating headline 'My price or out you go'. The list was: 1. tax reform involving income tax cuts; 2. employee profit-sharing; 3. help for small businesses and self-employed; 4. reform of Official Secrets Act; 5. grants for first-time home buyers; 6. a national efficiency audit; 7. a youth employment programme; 8. better consumer protection by strengthening Monopolies Commission; 9. assemblies for Scotland and Wales with a PR option; 10. progress on European elections, also by PR if possible. *The Guardian* rightly commented that 'the object of the exercise was not to force unacceptable legislation on the Labour Party but to arrive at some sensible arrangement about Bills which could be agreed between the two parties and which would never reach the statute book without such an agreement'.

In addition to the ten points there were four important provisos for a further agreement: 1. the pay policy must be effective; 2. we must be consulted in advance on the form of government proposals unforeseen at present; 3. there should be less secrecy and more openness on the agreement; 4. we would not support further cuts in defence spending.

On Monday afternoon I went as arranged after our meeting to see the Prime Minister. We swopped accounts of our weekends. He told me that even his four original dissenters in the cabinet (Benn,

Booth, Orme and Millan) had come round to accepting the agreement. Benn had said, 'we want no quitting, no splitting and no losing'. I recorded in my diary:

> Chequers weekend full of Healey's optimistic forecasts. I said ours ditto with Pardoe's. He says we must watch these two or they'll give everything away in tax cuts!

I told him that the agreement was working patchily with some ministers not entering properly into the spirit of it. He asked for names and promised to have a word in their ears. I suggested not yet as we had to make a bigger effort on our side first.

I suggested that any new agreement should go to the Parliamentary Labour Party for them to consider and feel more involved in. He said he would think about this as possibly a good idea. We discussed the ten points and he vetoed none.

Unlike the last meeting we were in good mood and talked for nearly an hour. He made one rather odd suggestion of possible joint opinion polling of the public on specific issues, an idea which I said we could think about though we were short of money. Neither of us ever pursued this.

Later I talked to the lobby on our weekend and the proposals for next day's press. We led the TV news bulletins that evening.

The next day with its full press coverage coincided with the jubilee naval review at Spithead, which took place in a dull drizzle. I found myself on a ship behind the royal yacht with four of the cabinet, Elwyn-Jones, Mason, Peart and Barnett, all of whom seemed happy with the published proposals as we passed a rather tedious and chilly day in food and drink.

Just a week later, Tuesday 5 July, I went to the by-election at Saffron Walden, where I was encouraged to find our candidate taking an effective and aggressive pro-pact stance. I found on calling round the council estates on the doorstep during the afternoon that Labour voters were as a result prepared to switch to Liberal in second place in this Tory seat. One man even said to me: 'You've made our lot a better government and I'll vote for you this time because we've no chance.' In the evening I made a speech dismissed by the *Daily Telegraph* next day as 'an exercise in sabre rattling designed to convince the voters on polling day tomorrow that the Liberals are prepared to use their influence on the government'.

In fact it was also designed to reinforce our view that a firm pay policy was a *sine qua non* of renewal of the agreement. The National Union of Mineworkers' conference had overturned their leader's decision to abide by the TUC restraint policy. I said, 'we have a right to expect the government to stand firm on behalf of us all against any one greedy pressure group'. John Pardoe elsewhere in the constituency dovetailed his speech and declared that the Liberal Party 'is not going to underwrite a pay explosion'.

On Wednesday the Transport Union also voted against their leader Jack Jones and the TUC policy, and on Thursday *The Times's* first leader was headed 'Little chance for Phase Three'. Thursday was polling day at Saffron Walden. (It revived anxious memories for me because the Liberal candidate had lost his deposit in the by-election in the same constituency in 1965 the day before my own by-election victory.) I was having lunch in the members' dining room when I received a message asking me to return to my office to take an urgent telephone call from the Prime Minister. My diary records:

> JC telephoned to tell me of the morning's cabinet meeting. First time he has ever phoned himself. Yesterday's vote by the TGWU following that of the NUM against a Phase III pay deal has obviously put the cat among the pigeons. He says Healey will meet TUC economic committee on Tuesday, and cabinet will approve a new economic statement next Thursday.
>
> I point out that without a TUC agreement or statutory control he will be left with the Tory policies of cash limits in the public sector and the spectre of greater unemployment.
>
> 6.30 pm. I decided to see PM to ask whether any prospect of statutory enforcement of twelve-month pay increase gap. He rules it out emphatically but agrees to ask TUC economic committee to renew endorsement of it for inclusion in the government's white paper.
>
> I point out that I have made numerous speeches on importance of pay deal and absence of 'window dressing' and that if they rely totally on the same policies as the Tories we shall be asked: 'why bother to support Labour?' He says genially that that is my problem, which indeed it is.
>
> We then discuss timetable for a new agreement and he says he wants it by the end of July.

He complains that Shirley Williams hasn't been able to get Alan Beith to discuss her education paper, and will I jolt him. Asks after likely result in Saffron Walden and whether I am getting a summer holiday. We part in good humour, but the outlook is gloomy.

Friday brought good news with the result of the by-election at Saffron Walden. On a reduced poll the Tory vote was up 1,000 but we held second place comfortably on a reduced vote of 251, while Labour slumped. Most newspapers correctly guessed this would help the renewal of the agreement, but the *Economist* rightly kept to the main issue: 'Mr Steel would prefer to renew it, but he will be under pressure at the party conference in September to end it if the pay policy is already in rude tatters.'

Early in July John Mackintosh was taken suddenly ill in the first of his two bouts of illness which were to lead to his tragic death. He wrote to me from his bed with wise words of advice:

> Nether Liberton House,
> Edinburgh,
> 1st July [1977]

Dear David,

While prone on my back, I have thought a lot about you and your situation as I am sure it is vital for everyone that you and the Liberal Party come out of all this as well as possible and it is a crucial situation. So herewith my reflections:—

1. I do not think, after my PLP attendances, that the Pact has had any deep effect on the Lab. Party and *even if* the economic indicators do turn up, I think the Party will be a pretty shambolic government next session. I cannot see the electorate saying in late '78 or early '79, 'this has been a sufficiently coherent and good government for us to thank you, Mr Steel, for keeping them in power. In gratitude we will vote Liberal.'

2. To have run the pact thus far has left you with a separate identity but if you vote with the LP time and again for another 18 or 12 months, this will disappear. You will become a joint in the Labour tail. You will face the irritation that Labour rebellions will get more headlines and some concessions while you have to loyally vote with the Government. At the election,

you can make no attack on Labour – or else how can you justify keeping them in power for such a long period?

So I think you should get off the hook this coming winter or autumn. Where Jim Callaghan has pushed you into a corner is by asking for a commitment *this July* for a whole session ahead. So you produce your 10 point programme and Jim will huff and puff a bit for the sake of the left but will more or less agree, Labour leaders having been accepting programmes for years from the left and then doing very little about it. If you agree and sign up, every time something does not come off – endless debates on direct elections etc. (remember, the opponents will have a further Labour Party Annual Conference vote behind them) – you will wonder whether to go with the Pact but Jim will suggest that this is a minor point and that if you want to change your mind, it reveals that you made an error of judgement in signing up for a whole session. In short, the issue will not be the merits of his government but your sagacity and position as Leader of the Liberal Party.

I believe you must not be pushed into this corner and you must have it clear that if and when you want to break off the Pact, it is *Jim's fault* and you must have a clear issue or issues on which to attack him in the election.

The way to do this (and it is one the public would understand) is to say 'I cannot sign a pact in July for a whole session because I have no confidence that the Labour Party can deliver. I ask for 10 points in the Queen's speech but the Pact will depend *not on promises but on delivery*. If the Government, at any time, fail to deliver on (say) any one of four or five crucial points, the deal is off. These points are (just possibilities) 1. United Cabinet support for Direct Elections once the principle is approved this summer. 2. A guillotine on devolution. 3. A 10% norm on pay settlements. 4. Shift to indirect taxation in the Budget. 5. A revised 'Bullock' Bill.

The points should be quite specific so it is clear when they are broken. If the Government carry them, you get some credit, if they fail on any one, you can say 'it's the Government's fault. They could not deliver. We must have an election with Liberalism a positive, distinct alternative to this shambolic coalition in the Labour Party and the unknown rightwingism of a Thatcher regime.'

Sorry to go on so long but illness leaves the mind time to contemplate. Come in for a meal anytime you are passing this weekend or next or we could have a chat in London. Love to Judy.

Yours ever,
John

At our next weekly meeting on Wednesday 13 July the shadow administration was due to report back and consider all the contacts with ministers on the ten-point renewal programme, on the eve of the cabinet's deliberations on pay policy. Everyone duly reported on their negotiations with their opposite numbers. Jo Grimond enlivened the proceedings with a hilarious account of eating five biscuits over tea with Tony Benn while discussing some new electricity Bill Benn was keen to introduce.

One delicate constitutional issue arose out of the blue. I had intended to discuss at some point with Frank Byers the tricky question of who would actually decide whether or not the agreement was renewed – would the peers have a say? But 'delicacy' and 'tact' are not words that appear in Cyril Smith's dictionary. He has a down-to-earth and attractive blunt northernness which at times can be upsetting. I noted in my diary that it was a difficult meeting:

> Cyril wades in and demands to know who will have the right to decide by vote on whether the Lib–Lab agreement goes on. Naturally I have to rule that it would be the MPs only, though the views of the peers in the team would have to be taken into account. Rather tired and phrased myself badly. The peers like Desmond Banks and Nancy Seear, who have been doing a lot of work, explode and demand that the views of the whole shadow administration be taken first. George Mackie proclaims that they don't mind being treated as second-class citizens but object to Cyril regarding them as third-class.

During the day there were various phone calls to and from Number Ten with my asking to see the proposed economic white paper in draft. I asked John Pardoe to see Healey as well to discuss it.

After the party meeting, Russell Johnston and George Mackie

came to my room to brief me on the outcome of their long series of talks with the government on a new devolution package:

> Hardly started when I am summoned along the corridor by Michael Foot. He is with John Smith [minister in charge of devolution] and warns me that Johnston and Mackie are upset on some points because John Smith had no authority to negotiate further. Foot wants me to know that he and I can still discuss any disagreements further. I find this irritating because it all lands back in my lap.

Thursday 14 July was the date of the cabinet's discussion of the new economic package:

> During the morning Ken Stowe telephones to say that the PM had seen the white paper that morning and that it was 'no bloody good' and not therefore to be sent to me. Cabinet still discussing. After lunch he rings again to say they've decided not to have a white paper at all, but just Healey's statement tomorrow. I'll have final draft after the evening cabinet. We agree not necessary to meet PM since Healey due to discuss with Pardoe in the evening.
>
> Later Pardoe came to my room to report on talks with Healey. Very unsatisfactory. No firm pay agreement, and Healey withholds specific information on grounds that Pardoe is not a Privy Counsellor. Only I am to receive full briefing. This is very annoying again because it falls back on me. I get the full text after dinner and discuss it with John whose guidance I require. We both find it depressing, and I collar Roy Hattersley into my room to explain one paragraph I simply do not understand. The lesson is not helped by the fact that it turns out he is working from the earlier cabinet draft in his pocket, whereas I have the post-cabinet version. I take the chance of telling him that I asked our peers whom I met earlier to try to strengthen his prices Bill in the Lords on Monday. JC speaks to me in the corridor on his way to the dining room and again in the division lobby, on both occasions for several minutes in full view of passing MPs. He seems to rate reassuring me that he still has some policy left as higher than his usual demands of secrecy about our meetings.

Friday morning saw Healey making his statement to the Commons. I had left John Pardoe to deal with it and travelled overnight to Dundee to see my father receive an honorary degree from the university. When I arrived both university officials and press were in a state of nerves because I had been asked to take a call from Number Ten. It was simply to tell me of last-minute out unimportant alterations in Healey's text.

The Guardian summed up the Healey package of tax and price cuts as 'trying to cajole the British public with its own money into accepting another year of pay restraint . . . politically the main question is where the package leaves the Lib–Lab pact'. John Pardoe said in the House that the package's success depended on the way the government reacted to the first big pay claims.

The following Monday I was attending a ceremony at Lambeth Palace for the twentieth anniversary of the Civic Trust. I arranged to leave early after the Prime Minister and meet him back in his room at 4pm.

I told him that in the light of Healey's statement we could not guarantee support till autumn 1978 as we had been considering because there was no certainty that the policy would work. Nor was I keen on short-term month-to-month agreements. I thought we should still try to agree a common programme for next session and support it so long as inflation was controlled. He agrees we will have to think over the wording carefully.

He also indicates that the twelve-month gap between pay rises will be held by the TUC, and he will have to face strikes balancing the cost of not giving in against the damage to counter-inflation policy if he does. He sounds a lot tougher in private than in public utterances and I urge him to take that line in Wednesday's debate on the package.

4.40pm. A quick meeting with Michael Foot urging him to put PR in a schedule to the Scottish and Welsh Bills, but he is not very responsive.

5pm. A rather bad meeting of the shadow administration in which great gloom is expressed about the economic outlook in the absence of a TUC agreement. We agree to support the government on Wednesday on the basis of the existing agreement, but Jo and David Penhaligon increasingly restless, Jeremy sounding anxious and John not at all happy.

Afterwards I rang Number Ten to urge more specific statements on Wednesday about controlling pay in the public sector and follow this up by letter.

Next day I had a good meeting with Russell Johnston, Michael Foot and John Smith to agree the finishing touches to the new devolution proposals. Some rewording of the revised financial provisions was agreed and Smith suggested 'First Secretary' as the title for the Scottish premier which is close to my 'First Minister' suggestion at Aviemore. Russell and George Mackie had done a very workmanlike reconstruction of the devolution package with John Smith.

In the evening we dined as a group with Len Murray, the general secretary of the TUC. He and I had decided on this when we met some weeks before but the time was happily fortuitous. We had a very relaxed evening beginning with David Penhaligon brandishing the *Evening Standard* with its headline about the British Steel Corporation, 'Steel loses 1 million a day', and asking devilishly 'Is that pounds or votes?' Most of the MPs had not met Murray before and were obviously impressed. What was vital was his emphasis on our shared objective of defeating inflation as priority number one, and his explanation of the difficulties the TUC had and would overcome to do this.

In Wednesday's debate Thatcher's lack of positive alternatives showed clearly. When I tackled her on this she said, 'Mr Speaker, if I may say through you to this young man. . . .' That helped to stiffen the troops.

On Thursday 21 July Ken Stowe phoned to fix a meeting with the PM for Monday 25th so that we could go through a proposed draft agreement for me to put to colleagues on Tuesday so that we could release the result before the summer recess. My press-named 'ten commandments' have become known as the 'thirty-nine articles' because of the proliferation of suggestions. The PM agreed to let me have his own briefing on the policy matters and a copy was sent round for me to take away for the weekend 'for my eyes only'. I also had a very brief meeting with Foot to approve the post-cabinet devolution statement. I did so quickly making one drafting amendment and one change of presentation.

The weekend press is full of copious advice. The *News of the World* plumbs a new depth in anti-Liberal nastiness by one columnist who suggests we should use Norman Scott in a party political broadcast instead of Jeremy Thorpe as we did last week. I spend the weekend mulling over Callaghan's document

SIDE BY SIDE

and drawing up my own balance sheet of advantages and disadvantages. I drafted the first version of my proposed renewal letter and showed it to the PM on Monday.

Ken Stowe then returned the text with suggested amendments and I put this to the parliamentary party next day. We came and went a bit on details but the principle was agreed, over two days (Grimond and Smith dissenting). The opening paragraph was vital, linking the duration of the agreement not to any fixed period but to success in counter-inflation policy, much as John Mackintosh had urged on me. The new devolution package was announced to the Commons on Tuesday, which helped the climate in the party, and on Wednesday we continued to put the finishing touches to the agreed letter, the PM showing me his draft reply for comment.

Late at night I penned a personal letter to the Prime Minister:

Dear Jim,
    I enclose my official letter for relaying to your colleagues and publication.

May I thank you very warmly for your patience and understanding during what has been a rather novel constitutional experiment, and for your kindness to me personally.

I do hope we achieve success in these endeavours, and meantime I wish you as peaceful and restful a summer recess as
possible.

Yours ever,
David

He replied next day with a similar handwritten note. The agreement therefore continued, the next storm clouds being the party
conferences and the TUC congress with possible collapse of the pay
policy.

The official letters exchanged were as follows:

27 July '77

Dear Prime Minister,

On 23rd March the Parliamentary Liberal Party agreed to
work with the Government for the remainder of the Parliamentary Session in the pursuit of economic recovery. Having
reviewed the operation of this agreement, we have decided to
continue co-operation into the next Session of Parliament for
so long as the objectives set out in the Chancellor's statement
of 15th July are sustained by the Government.

We are agreed that the fight against inflation and unemployment is of paramount national importance, and stress
the need for both the 12-month gap between pay increases and
the limit on the general level of earnings increase to 10%. The
Liberal Party has already supported the Government in both
Houses to secure the passage of the Price Commission Bill.

We agree to continue the consultative machinery, repeating
the proviso that this does not commit the Government to
accepting the views of the Liberal Party, nor the Liberal Party
to supporting the Government on any issue.

We understand that in the next Session of Parliament:

–the Government in tackling unemployment, which must
be a top economic and social priority, will place particular
emphasis on the problem of school leavers, and the potential
for increased employment amongst small businesses. The
Government has undertaken to investigate urgently further

short-term measures to reduce teacher unemployment. We have urged the Government to initiate an all-Party appeal to employers and Trade Unions to use the employment opportunities which are currently offered to them to help young people, with emphasis on apprenticeship and other forms of training.

– the Government has agreed to consider ways of encouraging the creation of schemes for profit sharing in private industry with a view to legislation.

– so far as is permitted within the economic strategy there should be a shift within the overall level of taxation away from taxes on incomes, while providing a level of public expenditure that will meet social needs.

– the Government will reintroduce the European Assembly Elections Bill and use its best endeavours to secure its passage through all stages in time to meet the Community's target date for holding such elections.

– new legislation for devolution to Scotland and Wales will be promoted in accordance with the statement by the Lord President on Tuesday, 23rd July.

– the Government will introduce legislation to provide help for first-time buyers, on the lines suggested in the Government's Green Paper on Housing Policy.

– the Government will bring forward proposals for a more effective competition policy and for greater consumer protection.

–the Government will continue its consultations with the Liberal Party, already begun, with a view to determining the priorities in the Queen's Speech, and on such other matters as the provision of legal assistance at major public enquiries, stricter scrutiny of public expenditure and reform of the Official Secrets Act.

Yours sincerely,
David Steel

Dear David,

Thank you for your letter of 27 July telling me that the Liberal Party have decided to continue in the next session of Parliament our agreement to work together for the purpose of economic recovery.

I reaffirm that the fight against inflation and unemployment will continue as a first priority and I welcome the support of the Liberal Party in Parliament for policies to secure those objectives.

I agree that we should continue the consultative arrangements which we established earlier this year, and which have worked well. These arrangements will preserve the independence and integrity of each of our Parties, whilst enabling us to work together in the next session of Parliament.

I confirm the Government's position on the particular issues and proposals to which you refer in your letter and agree that we should continue consultations already begun about other possible measures that might be brought forward in the next session.

I am grateful for the co-operation of the Liberal Party. The stability provided by your support in Parliament has enabled the Government and the country to make progress towards the economic recovery on which the future prosperity of our people depends.

Yours sincerely,
Jim Callaghan

Chapter 7

The Brighton Conference and the Queen's Speech

The summer recess passed peacefully until mid-September when the conference season began with the TUC followed by ourselves a week later than usual and resulting in some overlap with Labour's National Executive pre-conference meeting in the same town – Brighton.

On 15 September I had a meeting with Michael Foot to start the process of agreeing the programme for the new session of parliament for inclusion in the Queen's Speech. For some time we had discussed strengthening the machinery of the agreement if it was to proceed on a longer-term basis than its original four months. He introduced me to the civil servant, Carolyn Morrison, who was being seconded from the Civil Service Department to run the agreement and be secretary to the consultative committee. She was to prove invaluable in a liaison role with all government departments. At the same time I had persuaded my former personal assistant Archy Kirkwood to take a year's leave of absence from his legal practice in the Borders to accept a new appointment as 'Head of the leader's office' with particular responsibility for co-ordinating our side of the agreement. I had also pointed out the overcrowded and chaotic nature of my office in the House and pleaded unsuccessfully to be found larger premises. I did, though, get a long loan of an extra room for a secretary and filing across the road in the Norman Shaw building. I wrote in my diary:

> I stress again the need to have something new to tell the Liberal Assembly and I show him the draft I have sent over to Denis Healey of what I would like to say about the government's plans on profit sharing. He says leave it to Denis to approve.

Next day I followed this up in a lengthy meeting with the Prime Minister, and recorded the mood as follows:

One of the longest and most relaxed meetings so far with the PM. Started at 10am and lasted an hour, in Number Ten (entry by the front door this time). 'Sunny Jim' certainly living up to his nickname. He began by asking if I'd had a good holiday and waxed lyrical about his own visit to Scotland.

Then he asked me about my visit to Nigeria for the United Nations anti-apartheid conference. (I wondered how much he knew of the awkwardness at the Lagos conference where an embarrassed Frank Judd – Minister of State at the FCO – and I had exchanged previews of our speeches: his was circumscribed by cautious official policy towards southern Africa while mine was more blunt and to Judd's liking.) We compared notes on Nigerian politicians before getting down to business.

I asked about the prospects of holding wage claims, and he was both optimistic and determined after the TUC vote. He had done quite a bit of lobbying before the conference.

I repeated my wish to have something to tell our assembly in advance of the Queen's Speech to help swing the vote behind the pro-agreement resolution. I stressed the profit-sharing point and he had a copy of Healey's letter to me in his brief. He slightly demurred at Healey's commitment to the Finance Bill because he wants a short one to 'clear the decks' for a possible election. I told him I thought it would only need one clause.

At this point he went off at a tangent to say he was thinking of October 1978 or Spring 1979 as the real election options, and that he thought it only right to keep me informed as to his thinking. This was most unexpected. He said he therefore wanted items with 'sex appeal' in the legislative programme and produced an enormous list of possibles from Sir John Hunt, Secretary to the Cabinet. We agreed that before the legislation committee of the cabinet distilled this I should have a detailed discussion with Michael Foot, and that thereafter and before the final cabinet decisions there should be a meeting of the consultative committee to go over the Queen's Speech content.

On direct elections he said ministers would have as free a vote as anyone. He thought the majority were against the regional list. I made a mental note to step up our lobbying on this issue among ministers.

I asked about possible reflation in the autumn, and about help for small businesses to boost employment. He agrees that this is desirable and says Harold Lever is looking at this. He is also keen on stimulating the construction industry, and announcing prospective tax cuts, especially the reintroduction of a reduced rate band. ('Roy Jenkins didn't understand the effect it would have when he abolished it.')

I told him I would say something about the use of North Sea oil revenues in my assembly speech on the Saturday.

I asked about the life peerages list which was to come in the autumn. He said he hadn't turned his mind to it yet, but I could suggest names. I said I would rather not until I knew the nature of the list and the number we would have. We had an amusing exchange in which he confirmed that he would ask the Tories to nominate and that he would be topping up the Labour strength. He had thought it wise to let time elapse since Harold's last list. I told him I kept coming across people half-promised peerages by Jeremy, and we agreed both had enjoyed this side of life while we regarded it as a source of trouble and discontent. We both marvel at the number of volunteers we receive to 'serve in the upper house'.

Then we reviewed the political situation. He is bucked by the Gallup poll showing the Tory lead down to $4\frac{1}{2}$ per cent and summons Tom McNally to bring in other polls – one to be published by the *Sunday Times*. He regales me with extracts including standing of the leaders and the fact that on issues Liberal and Labour views are closer than Tory ones. In fact profit-sharing is very popular among Labour voters which I note with particular interest.

He asks if I will take the line that we will be willing to join the Tories after an election and I say I see no alternative but to keep this balance. He says he doesn't see Labour candidates standing down in third places – they tend to be extreme there, but it sounds as though he is giving a lot of thought to possible Labour victory.

We talked about the Labour NEC meeting at the Grand Hotel, Brighton, on the Friday of our assembly. He thinks it not a good idea for him to have a drink with me, but says we should meet. I suggest we get Joan Lestor as Labour chairman to invite us both. He says she might not be willing 'with one eye on her votes for the executive' but we leave it that I would approach her. If not, we'll arrange a routine meeting.

Later I phone Joan Lestor who agrees to a Friday lunchtime drink.

In the week prior to the Liberal conference I made one positive advance on profit-sharing and received one setback in failing to secure Liberal credit for Harold Lever's appointment to oversee the interests of small businesses, something my colleagues had been assiduously pressing. My diary outlined the sequence of events on Wednesday 21 and Thursday 22 September when I was at home in Ettrick Bridge.

Wednesday 21 September 1977

A letter comes round to the office from Joel Barnett about four o'clock replying on behalf of Denis Healey (who is abroad) and agreeing the section of my speech to the assembly about profit-sharing, with drafting alterations which leave it much too weak. Also a PS on small businesses enclosing a press handout from Number Ten issued earlier in the day. It is all read over the phone to me at home and I suggest a rushed press comment approving Harold Lever's appointment to take charge of a study across government departments of the needs of small businesses. This is very much what Callaghan and I had discussed the previous week. I know I asked them to speed things up before the assembly, but there has been a lamentable lack of warning.

I ring Number Ten but JC together with Ken Stowe and Tom McCaffrey, the press officer, are on an official visit to Rome. I then discover a monumental cock-up on our part, stemming from the physical separation of my office into two parts. An official had rung from Number Ten at 9.45 that morning to 'my office' (actually Alistair Michie's phone in the whip's office). He wasn't there and the call was taken by a girl on the whip's office staff. The message was that the small business announcement was going to be made later in the morning and the press notice was on its way over. The actual press release came by messenger to my own office, who had no knowledge of its coming or significance and transferred it to Alistair Michie's tray in the whip's office later in the day.

It is partly all their faults, but really one cannot run an efficient office in these conditions.

Thursday 22 September 1977

We get no credit for the small business announcement. Beith, Wainwright and Howells are furious, though I point out that it is partly our own fault. However, Downing Street should have given us longer notice to agree the statement even if they didn't actually refer to us in it and I agree to pursue the matter.

Joel Barnett is tracked down to Sussex and I speak to him on the telephone. I told him his redrafting was unacceptably feeble in referring to profit-sharing changes that 'could' be in next year's Finance Bill. He agrees to my changing this to 'will'.

On Monday 26th before setting off for Brighton I had a further meeting with Michael Foot, to go through all the twenty-three possible bills for next session (see Appendix 2 for official note).

On Tuesday I opened the conference contrary to the usual practice of just delivering a leader's speech on the last day. I naturally wanted to set out our record and the way ahead as I saw it before the party's strategy debate on Wednesday. I produced all the arguments in favour of the course we had taken and they went down quite well:

We therefore agreed that our decision should depend on the terms the Prime Minister would publicly agree in order to ensure maintenance of the government and on the creation of machinery to assist Liberal influence over it for the remainder of the parliamentary session.

Let's not exaggerate what can be achieved by the influence of thirteen MPs on a party of over three hundred MPs. Every day I receive letters – some hostile to the agreement, others friendly to it – which advise me to break it off if the government does (or fails to do) such and such. The list of potential breaking points becomes enormous. Let us face the fact squarely that 'we are in the position of a body of men whose sole sanction to enforce their behests is capital punishment. There are two objections to that. You cannot inflict capital punishment for minor offences; and you can only inflict it once for any offence.' These are not my words but those of David Lloyd George in 1931.

Our influence through this limited agreement has so far been largely but not unimportantly negative. We can and have stopped nationalization; we can and did stop certain tax proposals, thus reducing petrol tax and freeing thousands of small businesses from VAT; we can and will oppose those cuts in defence spending which would take us below our obligations to collective security in NATO; we stemmed the flow of partisan legislation.

But our influence has been positive as well. Foremost we have made a major political contribution to national stability and recovery over the last six months. As the director-general of the CBI [Confederation of British Industry] put it earlier this month: 'at least businessmen have returned to operating in a climate in which they can plan ahead – instead of reacting to circumstances on a week-by-week basis'.

But my trump card as I thought was the commitment on profit-sharing. To my dismay the assembly did not seem to grasp what I was saying, or else I put it badly in a speech that was too long and detailed. At any rate, the passage was brilliantly lampooned by James Fenton, the political columnist of the *New Statesman*, on the Friday:

The fact was that, although Steel was appreciatively heard, nobody was actually listening to a word he was saying. They were listening to the cadences. They were waiting for the emphases. They were enjoying the climaxes. They were not thinking about the content, largely because, in all the years they have been Liberals, they have never expected to hear a speech with any content. Content is not really what they're interested in. If they were, they wouldn't be Liberals. Steel has managed to extract from the Government a promise that they would put something about profit-sharing in the next Finance Bill. And not only that, he had gone to great lengths to get permission to announce this himself, so that no one would be in any doubt that this was a Liberal measure. The whole of his speech was conducted in such a way as to lead up to this announcement – look boys, here we are, we've actually got something. Pause. I said we've actually got something. Pause. Did you hear? It's really true, after all these years we've done something towards profit-sharing – for crying out loud it's going to be in the next Finance Bill. Applause.

Old habits of thought die hard, and the old habit of Liberal thought is abstract hope, a hope that, like Hamlet's chameleon, eats the air, promise-crammed. Liberal thought is not used to discussions of tactics or deals. It finds it difficult to concentrate on the present day. It finds it difficult to concentrate, period. That is why Steel, in addressing the party, has the air of a teacher, but a teacher whose points are continually being missed. What was that he said, for instance about a coalition? 'Now we have to demonstrate that if this much can be done by a tiny band of Liberals outside the Government, how much more could be done by a larger group inside the next Government ...' Did he really say that? What does it mean?

Late that night I had to telephone the Swedish Liberal leader and Deputy Prime Minister Per Ahlmark and apologize for repeating unscripted an unflattering crack he had made to me about his Tory coalition partner in the government, which had been relayed back to Sweden, to his embarrassment.

The strategy debate itself went well next day and was of a very high standard. The assembly passed a resolution declaring its support for the agreement and rejecting an amendment calling for its renegotiation by 716 votes to 385. Cyril Smith who had backed the amendment resigned his employment spokesmanship later that day. Jo Grimond had already asked to be relieved of shadowing Benn. Greater damage to party unity had lain in an amendment demanding a majority of at least a hundred in the Parliamentary Labour Party for PR in the European elections as a condition for staying in the agreement. I managed to persuade Chris Mayhew, the mover, to water it down to 'a substantial majority', but I was still uneasy when it was passed.

The next day, Thursday, I made two telephone calls from the conference, one to Michael Foot and one to Ken Stowe at Number Ten.

I telephone Foot to convey no objections to any items that we knew of, but I ask for a complete list with details on paper which I would chop up and send to each spokesman as appropriate. Foot agrees, but worried on security of such a list, because pre-cabinet. I said no one would see the lot except me.

Foot sounds cheerful about outcome of assembly debate on the agreement.

Phone K. Stowe and go over small businesses cock-up in detail. Agreed that I should convey apologies to Wainwright etc. I also raise prospective meeting with JC on Friday. I've gone off the idea of Joan Lestor as hostess because I intend to attack the Labour Party, especially the left, on Saturday and can hardly be seen fraternizing with her as chairman. K. Stowe consults PM and in a later call agrees we should have an ordinary business meeting. I phone J. Lestor who is much relieved since she has felt it inappropriate 'especially since many of the left believe JC told you to say certain things'. I don't know what she means, but it seems that I've got under their skin.

On Friday I had a much publicized meeting in the Grand Hotel with the Prime Minister who had arrived for his National Executive meeting:

Meet JC in his suite for coffee after lunch. He is very warm and complimentary about the assembly and says 'you looked very good on television' from which it appeared he may have been watching it live. He particularly liked my bit about the thirteen to three hundred. His suite is called 'The Napoleon' and mine 'The Helena' ('not "The Josephine" as you might expect', writes a *Guardian* wag). I told him of the way the debate had gone and said I was sure there was no need to reiterate the importance of PR for Europe in the eyes of the party.

He asks about the hitch on small businesses, but I assured him it was now all sorted out.

I told him of the departure of CS and JG from their shadow posts and that I would be appointing Nancy Seear and Eric Avebury in their places.

He asks if consultation going okay with Foot on Queen's Speech. I say everything under control, but would like mention of Co-operative Development Agency which was in Labour manifesto but seemed to be stuck somewhere. He is enthusiastic and agrees this should be brought forward.

He tells me of his letter to his own executive bringing them into line on the Common Market which is being released later. I told him I had already seen a copy and approved. He thought 'reform EEC from within' would steal a march on Thatcher, but I fear he overestimates the public impact of this. He is mainly heading off a split in his party.

He asks how my speech for tomorrow is going. I tell him pages are all over the floor. He says he is still looking at drafts for his and if I've any spare pages will I let him have them! He, surprisingly, shakes me warmly by the hand as I leave.

Bump into McNally outside who says we've disappointed lots of photographers lurking below. I said I'd just had a session with Judy and Rory on a fire engine ladder. He says JC will cap that by going out to part the waters between the piers.

The next day I delivered my wind-up speech to the conference. If Jim Callaghan had borrowed any pages it would not have done him much good because it was not a particularly coherent speech. It had been stitched together during the week together with bits I had prepared during the recess left over from the first speech, and the total prepared in a hectic week when my mind was on other things. I received a dutiful standing ovation (one of the by now obligatory yet irritating habits of these occasions) but resolved there and then not to make two speeches to the assembly in future. But I was pleasantly surprised to note:

> Return to the hotel immediately after my speech to be greeted enthusiastically by McNally and McCaffrey, the Number Ten press officer. As professionals they thought it went well. Mc-Nally says: 'He'll be asking us to produce something like that.'

The following Tuesday at home in Ettrick Bridge I watched Jim Callaghan on television live from his Brighton conference. Unexpectedly he went out of his way to thank me for my co-operation but reiterated as I had done that we fight the next election as independent parties, and that his aim is an overall majority.

The same day a long letter arrived from Carolyn Morrison with the list of Bills in detail (see Appendix 3). I literally chopped it up with scissors and pasted the relevant bits together for passing on to my colleagues with this advice in a letter:

> Between now and our meeting I hope you will discuss with your opposite number in the Government, the content of proposed Bills relating to your subject areas. I enclose details of Bills that relate to your subject areas and have notified other

colleagues who may have a direct interest in the appropriate Bills.

I hope that you will be able to come to the Shadow Administration meeting armed with advice as to what our reactions should be to these Bills and the appropriate priorities. In your negotiations with Ministers you should also put forward any legislative or administrative suggestions of your own.

At our last meeting, in the Pavilion at Brighton, I was asked to pursue the possibility of a Co-operative Development Agency Bill. I am glad to say that the Prime Minister is personally keen on this, though it has not so far appeared on the list sent to me by the Lord President.

Will you please take the chance to inquire privately about the voting intention of your Minister (and his departmental juniors) in the free vote on PR for Europe.

I think we must lobby on PR for Europe on a bilateral basis like this, rather than leave all the pressure to be applied via the Prime Minister.

At the same time I issued a press release announcing the reshuffle necessitated by Jo's and Cyril's reluctance to carry on working the agreement with Benn and Booth. It is unfortunate that they were teamed up with two of the original opponents and they have never worked happily in the agreement (see Appendix 4 for new list of appointments). Because peers were to take over employment and energy, David Penhaligon agreed to understudy their work in the Commons.

On Friday 7 October the formidable Baroness Seear had her first meeting with Albert Booth. The official note (see Appendix 5) accurately reflects our continuing concern with countering inflation as top priority in our open-ended agreement. She urged a firm government line on Ford's wage negotiations, and with the Transport and General Workers Union (TGWU) generally.

Later that week I had two further letters from Michael Foot on the continuing preparations for the Queen's Speech. Then on 18 October with the Commons meeting for the 'spillage' of the old session before the opening of the new one, we had a full-day meeting of the shadow administration when I recorded:

The shadow administration meets in Frank Byers's room in the Lords and we go over all the possible programme of legislation for next session. We decide to break at lunch and resume in the evening, when we agree our lines on the economic strategy.

The consultative committee meets in the afternoon and seems to go well. (See Appendix 6 for minute.)

The MPs all seem buoyant after the assembly and report that the opinion tide appears to have turned in favour of the agreement.

The next few days were occupied to my distraction with a fresh outbreak of press stories on the Thorpe–Scott affair which had lain mostly dormant since Jeremy's resignation as leader eighteen months previously. I noted the time-consuming sequence of events in my diary:

Wednesday 19 October 1977

Archy rings me at the flat to pass on a tip-off that the *Evening News* is resurrecting the Norman Scott affair. Sure enough, it does. JT is in Devon and we get him on the line mid-morning. He arranges to come back to London next morning. Newton is alleging that he was hired by 'a leading Liberal supporter' to kill Scott. The *Evening Standard* headline is 'Liberal's £5,000 murder plot', an obvious smear which requires careful noting of the apostrophe. The press hounds start up again and I advise 'no comment'.

Lunch at 10 Downing Street for the new Spanish premier. Donoughue and Stowe both express sympathy that this is all blowing up again – they know that the press are still trying to get at Harold Wilson, though what precisely he was trying to do in the JT troubles none of us know.

As I went in I was handed the seating plan for 'The Rt Hon. David Owen MP'. I spotted the mistake and pointed out to an embarrassed aide that I was not the Foreign Secretary. Owen asks if I have issued a statement on South Africa (they have just banned a newspaper and a whole lot of bodies and individuals). I have to admit that the Scott affair has distracted me from doing so: it is really so annoying and time-consuming.

Healey cheerfully says: 'I see you've written my budget for me' (a reference to our shopping list in the morning papers). Jack Jones and Len Murray are both affable and Murray asks to see me soon for a talk.

At 6pm I am on *Nationwide* 'on the spot' answering questions from viewers. The Norman Scott thing could not have broken on a worse day and I have inevitably to deal with it first. I express dismay and say I don't know who the alleged hirer of the killer is supposed to be.

Thursday 20 October 1977

A hellish day. All the pop papers lead on the Scott story. 'A top Liberal', 'a prominent Liberal' and 'a leading Liberal' are mentioned variously. Bessell has surfaced again and says such a fantasy plot was discussed at 'Liberal meetings' which conveys an appalling impression. In the course of the day I learn from three different journalist sources that the man Newton is alleging hired him was David Holmes (an old friend of Jeremy's whom he had appointed as his assistant when party treasurer and a man totally unknown to most Liberals) and also that Bessell is saying his 'meetings' consisted of himself, JT and Holmes. The papers can't print any of this because of libel laws, but I am increasingly worried that the whole party is therefore being smeared. Emlyn thinks it is close to group libel and agrees that I should issue a statement to the effect that the party is not involved. I ask JT to come and see me because his house is surrounded by the press.

In the midst of all this turmoil I almost forgot I had to lunch with the governors of the BBC to talk to them informally. I arrive late and leave early and write to Michael Swann afterwards to apologize for being so distracted by other events.

John Macdonald QC, chairman of the Liberal lawyers, told me the previous day that he was being brought in by some Liberals to advise JT.

JT turns up in the late afternoon with Macdonald. He has accepted Macdonald's advice to tell all at a press conference. He won't tell me what 'all' is until he has cleared it with his lawyers.

I draft a statement which he agrees announcing the press conference early next week and adding in effect that the 'leading Liberal' allegedly involved is nothing of the kind.

In the midst of this I find time to phone Ken Stowe at Number Ten to relay various points to the PM on the budget, police pay, Ford wage negotiations, etc.

I decide to cancel my visit next Monday–Wednesday to Houston, Texas, for BCAL's inaugural flight using the Wednesday mini-budget as the excuse.

Friday 21 October 1977

A busy day out and about in the constituency. Alistair phones with the continuing press stories. He says Newton may be in Jersey with a Sunday newspaper and I agree he should phone the Home Office to urge that he be not allowed to leave the country until investigated by the police.

Saturday 22 October 1977

A pleasant day at home. John Mackintosh and family come to lunch and we risk our necks in the canoe on the river which is running high.

John Macdonald telephones in the middle of our lunch and Emlyn Hooson soon afterwards both anxious about the legal and political implications of the press stories.

Monday 24 October 1977

Having cancelled my trip to Houston I went to see Merlyn Rees. He is in the new Home Office building which looks like a South American dictator's last fortress. His high glass office looks out on St James's Park and he beckons me to the window to watch the guards marching past. It is a magnificent view but somehow the whole place lacks the character of the Home Secretary's old office.

We quickly agree that it is really for the Attorney General to see that the police inquiries are speeded up. He points out that the lurid press speculation about intervention of previous Home Secretaries must be wide of the mark because although people like to indulge in such fantasies, Home Secretaries have very little power on such matters. He undertakes to pass on to Silkin my request that inquiries be speeded up and efficiently conducted at the highest level. He says the detective superintendent in charge is very competent and is high powered.

We go on to discuss police pay. I tell him we are keen to see any device used to secure a settlement which does not breach the 10 per cent guideline, because the Tories are building up a head of steam for the police to be a special case. Rees agrees that this is what he will be trying to do next day.

He asks me about immigration. He proposes to extend the scope of the amnesty on illegal immigrants but bring it to an end on a specific date next year. There may be a Tory reaction, but I think he is right and say so with the proviso that Eric Avebury should be consulted as our spokesman.

In the evening I invite myself round with Clement Freud to Jeremy's house, dodging in through the back door to avoid photographers.

The next day the consultative committee met again and after a lengthy discussion which included Shirley Williams and her advisers on a scheme to reduce unemployment among school-teachers, they tackled other outstanding matters (recorded in Appendix 7).

On Wednesday 2 November I had my final meeting with the Prime Minister prior to next day's state opening:

I go to see JC at Number Ten entering via the cabinet office and the connecting door at their request.

We discuss the text of the Queen's Speech, the formal version of which I got that morning. I told him I was concerned about the vagueness of the section of profit-sharing, but he said there was no intended dilution of the government's commitment.

He read me a few passages of what he intended to say including a generous tribute to us for our part in economic recovery. Did I approve? Yes indeed. Also a section on the European elections Bill making it clear that only the list system would bring them in time for next year. That is good, but I asked him if he would declare his own support for the PR system. He said he would in time, but not yet. I pressed him, but he said he had a few hurdles to clear first. He expected the second reading fairly quickly and the vote on the election method before Christmas.

On devolution I told him I agreed the suggested tactic of hitting the House with the two second reading votes and the timetable motions all in one week.

I was briefed to ask him about lack of progress on Liberal proposals for a national efficiency audit to cut out waste in the bureaucracy. He thinks it has no sex appeal 'beyond the Public Accounts Committee and a few city editors'. I am inclined to agree but don't say so, since I've yet to see this policy beloved by some of my colleagues spelt out with coherent proposals.

He stresses we should claim credit for the first-time home buyers Bill, and indeed gives it to us in his speech next day though it is excluded from *Hansard* thanks to an interruption from Eric Heffer.

We discuss the power cuts and the miners' ballot rejecting the Coal Board's productivity pay bonus scheme. He makes it clear that he intends to stick by the 10 per cent rule and the public will have to put up with inconvenience. I tell him we will back that line firmly.

I ask him if he has thought of pushing devolution through and holding the general election in June. He says he has ruled nothing out but doesn't think it possible to get devolution through till the end of July at the earliest.

When I leave it is pouring with rain. Oddly, therefore, I depart from the front door in the Prime Minister's own car to save calling mine round. Number Ten doesn't seem to have any consistent policy on my appearances!

The next day the approved text was duly read by Her Majesty from the throne in the House of Lords.

Chapter 8

The Great Devolution Debacle

It is necessary to break the chronological sequence of events to deal with the subject of devolution which ran before, during and after the pact as an issue both important in itself and vital when discussing parliamentary arithmetic. Continuing Gladstone's vision of 'home rule all round', Liberals have supported home rule for Scotland consistently since the beginning of the century. It was only the outbreak of the First World War which prevented the passage of a Liberal Bill for Scottish self-government. It had had its second reading on the floor of the House in 1913, and was part of a plan for a federal system of government within the whole of the United Kingdom and Ireland.

Despite a downturn in Liberal parliamentary fortunes, devolution to Scotland and to Wales and to the English regions has been a recurring theme in the political activities of Liberal MPs. Jo Grimond made his maiden speech on the subject in 1950. Labour and Conservative governments, however, have seen the subject differently and it was not until 1967, when Mrs Winnie Ewing won a first by-election for the Scottish National Party (SNP) in Hamilton – formerly a safe Labour seat – that the Labour government recognized that Scottish and Welsh nationalism could become a serious threat to their support in traditional Labour areas. They set up the Royal Commission on the Constitution in 1969. This reported as the Kilbrandon Commission in 1973, and recommended devolved assemblies with important responsibilities for Scotland and Wales, elected by proportional representation, and a reduction in the numbers of Scottish and Welsh MPs at Westminster.

At the February 1974 general election the nationalist party in Scotland returned seven MPs and the Welsh nationalists of Plaid Cymru two. The Wilson government, noting from its minority position that the nationalist threat had seriously increased, immediately committed itself to a form of devolution in a white paper published in September 1974, 'Democracy and Devolution: Proposals for Scotland and Wales', which included some but far from all the Kilbrandon recommendations. Although devolution within the United Kingdom would be a fundamental constitutional reform, the government considered it in isolation from other constitutional subjects such as the European Economic Community and reform of the House of Lords, of the electoral system or of local government. Since 1974 we had been urging them to hold a convention for discussions on the way in which the whole country was governed, but we had met with only a negative response.

After nationalist parliamentary strength increased at the October 1974 election to eleven in Scotland and three in Wales another white paper, 'Our Changing Democracy: Devolution to Scotland and Wales', was published in November 1975. This was the forerunner to the enormous Scotland and Wales Bill introduced at the end of 1976. This Bill was the subject of no consultation with the Liberals, the SNP or Plaid Cymru, the parties pledged to devolution of one degree or another. But because even this Bill was better than nothing it had the goodwill of the supporters of devolution and it passed its second reading comfortably. But in order to get the Bill on to the statute book there should have been time for discussion of all its main points on the floor of the House; this would have been ensured by the introduction of a timetable motion at this point before committee stage started. The government did not accept this. The Bill therefore lumbered to a halt in its parliamentary passage on 22 February 1977 when, part-way through committee stage, the government decided too late to introduce a guillotine which was lost by 312 votes to 283. In that debate I pointed out that by its inflexibility the government had been steadily losing the support of the real friends of devolution.

Without support from at least one other party no new devolution proposals were likely to get through. The government was in a minority position and not all its own supporters would follow it into the lobbies on this issue, so the Callaghan government, as it then was, conceded at last that consultations were inevitable. As I have already described, our talks on devolution were virtually the forerunner of the Lib–Lab pact itself.

Devolution proposals were therefore one of the corner-stones on which the Lib–Lab agreement was soon after built. The agreement itself stated 'progress must be made on legislation for devolution, and to this end consultations will begin on the detailed memorandum submitted by the Liberal party.... In any future debate on proportional representation for the devolved Assemblies there will be a free vote.'

Kilbrandon had unanimously recommended that the assembly members be elected by a method of proportional representation but this point had been consciously omitted in all the government proposals on devolution to Scotland and Wales. The late Professor John P. Mackintosh – a man with a lifelong commitment to devolution – made two attempts to introduce proportional representation into the devolution Bills. He secured all-party support for his proposal for an Additional Member System. The first, in January 1977 during the Scotland and Wales Bill committee stage, was lost by 244 votes to 62 (at 4.23am); that was before the Lib–Lab agreement. After it was made, I urged Michael Foot, Leader of the House, strongly to consider putting proportional representation into the new Scotland Bill and Wales Bill, and was intensely irritated when on 15 September he turned this down saying the government would make no recommendation on the system of election one way or the other.

John Mackintosh's second attempt to get assembly members elected by proportional representation took place during debate on the Scotland Bill in November 1977 but his proposal was turned down by 290 votes to 107; under the agreement there was supposed to be a government free vote this time but John Smith, Michael Foot's deputy at the Privy Council Office with responsibility for the devolution bills, made a pointed speech against the voting reform and ministers were whipped to vote against the amendment.

The House of Lords too tried to introduce proportional representation into the Scotland Bill. They approved an amendment along proportional representation lines and at a meeting with the Prime Minister on 10 April 1978 I asked him to consider this Lords proposal carefully and not to give me an answer right away as it would be the wrong one! He replied that if there was any evidence of a shift in opinion on the issue he would consider it. On 9 May at a meeting at which John Pardoe and Michael Foot were also present and we were discussing ending the Lib–Lab agreement I again put to them the possibility of encouraging adoption of proportional representation for Scotland following that Lords amendment by a government recommendation plus free vote when it came back to the Commons.

Then on 24 May the Prime Minister told John Pardoe and myself at another meeting with Michael Foot that proportional representation was not on; in truth we hadn't expected otherwise. At a late-night talk with Foot and Michael Cocks, the government chief whip, on 28 June, though there was no change in the government's position on proportional representation, it was agreed that when the Lords amendment came up time would be allowed for a rerun of the proportional representation debate and this time John Smith would refrain from making his 'anti' speech. The vote would be more genuine too: the MPs on the government payroll would not be whipped to vote against the reform. Cocks undertook to make the figures 'look a little more respectable' by producing more Labour supporters, which they did on 6 July when they went 363 to 155, thanks also to growing Tory support following the Lords' vote.

The referendums to consult the people of Scotland and Wales about the devolution proposals had been the single important concession which the government had made on their initial devolution proposals prior to the Lib–Lab agreement. The referendums were announced in a particularly offhand manner during the second reading of the Scotland and Wales Bill. Michael Foot had the referendum clause printed on the Commons order paper and that was that. He had not even discussed the clause with MPs of his own party who favoured holding the referendums. But having conceded the principle, the government refused to hold the referendums at any time during the course of the Bill's – and later Bills' – passage, but only permitted the expression of approval or disapproval of the Acts once they had been agreed by parliament. No provision was to be made for asking the people of Scotland or Wales what they thought about the bigger subject of independence itself, nor about proportional representation, despite the ideal opportunity presented.

When the Scotland and Wales Bill guillotine motion was lost, and the first Bill foundered, the views of the Scottish and Welsh people could have been taken immediately; it was a perfect occasion for guidance from the people to a government in difficulty but the government would not contemplate this.

There was more governmental co-operation later in the year. At a meeting on 2 November 1977 the Prime Minister proposed the tactic, which I agreed, of holding the second reading votes on the Scotland Bill and the Wales Bill and with the guillotine motions all in the same week. This was the procedure I had advocated at the time of the abortive Scotland and Wales Bill. I urged him to push the Bills through all their stages rapidly and hold a June 1978 election immediately after the Bills had been given Royal Assent, but the Prime Minister did not think it would be possible to complete the passage of the Bills before the end of July.

After both Bills had been successful on second reading and the timetable motions had gone through, I discussed the date of the referendums with Callaghan during an hour-long meeting on 28 November 1977 and put to him that if the referendums had to be held before the general election then that would be an ideal opportunity to include a question on independence, the answer to which would spike the nationalist guns. I myself favoured holding the referendums in November 1978 after an autumn election as a June election was not possible.

On the evening of 25 January 1978 after a dinner at 10 Downing Street I recorded in my diary:

> Then I return to vote on the Scotland Bill whose committee stage guillotine descends at 11pm. A crazy amendment is carried against the government despite our support demanding a 40 per cent 'yes' vote in the referendum. Then Jo's amendment on Orkney and Shetland is due on, but it is 10.40 and I see Walter Harrison [deputy government whip] and two or three others (including a couple of Scotnats) delaying in the lobby. I remonstrate with Walter and say he should allow Jo to make his speech: 'But he'll call a division and we'll lose,' replies Harrison.
>
> Eventually protests are made in the chamber about the delay. The chairman sends the Serjeant at Arms into the lobby and he reports a group of members unwilling to move. The vote is then declared and Jo just gets in his amendment. The House is so angry that he wins by 83 against the government.

On 1 February there were further alarms and excursions on the Bill's progress. I noted:

> A day of confusion and alarm. I am lunching with the *Financial Times* when Ann Dawson rings and asks if I will attend a meeting on devolution in Foot's office at 2.45pm. I agree. At 2.20 Carolyn Morrison rings and asks if I will come right away. I do, but am puzzled about the urgency.

This turns out to be related to a new clause of Jo's possibly to be reached that evening on Orkney and Shetland. John Smith and Foot are both willing to accept it provided we resist the Tory amendment to it. I suggest we send for Jo. He is duly summoned and Smith and Foot fetch Millan. An inconclusive discussion takes place at the end of which it seems unlikely the new clause will be reached (this turns out to be the case).

Then at 7.30 just when I was leaving for a quiet dinner with Nadir Dinshaw, whose friendship and inspiration I increasingly value, Foot asks to see me again. This time alone, and he is distraught because Russell Johnston has just indicated in the House support for a Tory new clause to establish a bill of rights as part of the Scottish Constitution due to be voted on at 9pm. Foot says they will lose and this will further mess up the Bill and endanger third reading. I had left Alan Beith and Russell to sort this out and they had decided to back the Tories. On balance I think they are right because a bill of rights for Scotland could pave the way for the UK. I decide to abandon my dinner and talk to Alan Beith and Russell. They rightly remind me that Foot himself is antagonistic to a bill of rights and this could explain why he was upset. Nevertheless we ought to have given the government longer notice of our intention to dissent and I point out we cannot go on having these last-minute alarms. By this time (after 8pm) most of the Libs are determined to support the bill of rights. I decide to absent myself diplomatically by going to the respite of my dinner after all. Russell abstains, stricken by conscience, and the government defeats the amendment by a majority of twenty-four. So why all the fuss?

When Callaghan and I met again to discuss the timing of the referendums, on 7 February, he asked once more whether I thought it best to hold these before or after an election and I urged holding them afterwards although, as the House had carried the amendment stipulating that if less than 40 per cent of those entitled to vote voted 'yes' then the government must ask parliament to repeal the Acts, there was something to be said for having them on the same day and so encouraging a high turn-out. He seemed interested in this possibility.

The referendum date came up for discussion again on 20 March

1978. The Prime Minister and I both agreed that the devolution Bills should be on the statute book before a general election was held and he also, at that time, accepted that the referendums should be held afterwards which I argued strongly pointed to October for the election.

At the end of September, after Callaghan had made his broadcast saying there would be no autumn election, much to my surprise and disappointment, he and I had our last meeting under the agreement. There I argued with some success for a late February or early March 1979 date for the referendums, so that the new electoral registers would be in use and the maximum number of people would have the opportunity to vote.

The Liberals believed that if the assemblies were to be both effective and responsible then they should have the power to raise some of their own income. If assemblies were set up with powers of expenditure but none of revenue raising, there must be trouble. Every worthwhile or worthy project not carried out could be blamed on the meanness of the Westminster government rather than on the intentions of the assembly members. An annual negotiation for a block grant from Westminster – the original government proposal – would mean an annual wrangle over cash.

Our original Scottish revenue-raising proposals to an early consultative committee meeting on 5 April 1977 were formulated by the Outer Circle Policy Group – an independent research group funded by the Joseph Rowntree Social Service Trust and headed by Professor James Cornford – which had on paper some things which we liked the look of at a time when we needed detailed proposals fast. Its contribution at this stage was knowledgeable and valuable. In all there were more than a dozen meetings of about three hours each between John Smith and the Liberal team headed by Russell Johnston, with George Mackie and Geraint Howells.

Our proposals for the royalties on North Sea oil to be available to the Scottish assembly, and for income tax collected in Scotland to go to the assembly which could vary the rate down or up (and thereby directly raise taxes for projects it advocated to the electorate from the electorate) were both rejected. But we managed in long negotiations to change the block grant from an annually agreed sum to a fixed percentage of United Kingdom expenditure, to be reviewed every four years. The government also agreed a statement of intent that they would consider any scheme of finance proposed by the assembly itself as long as the assembly was willing to meet the running costs of the scheme.

We had urged that the Welsh assembly should be financed by income tax raised in Wales, by 20 to 25 per cent of the petrol duty collected in Wales, and by an equalization grant. Although the overall sum would be the same as if it had all been one block grant, the psychological impact of spending a Westminster grant rather than revenue raised within Wales would be much reduced. These proposals proved in negotiation no more acceptable than our similar ones for Scotland and we finally accepted a change from the annually negotiated grant to the four-yearly negotiated grant which was a percentage of United Kingdom expenditure for Wales too.

Apart from the improved schemes for financing the assemblies, our other improvements to the government's devolution proposals included separate Bills for Scotland and for Wales instead of the joint one; a judicial review over the scope of the Scottish assembly legislation and a reduction in the powers of the Secretary of State for Scotland to override assembly legislation; and the title of the head of the assembly, once to have been Chief Executive with all its connotations of a high-ranking local government official, was changed to First Secretary.

On the reduction in the number of Scottish MPs at Westminster, a Kilbrandon proposal, and on the dissolution of a tier of local government, we got nowhere at all.

The Bills became Acts. The referendums were not held after an autumn 1978 election as I had hoped and advised, but on 1 March 1979, two months before the general election.

The result was a disaster. In Wales the proposals were defeated even more heavily than expected, and in Scotland they were approved by a bare majority of 33 per cent to 31 per cent, falling far short of the 40 per cent requirement. There were a number of reasons for this debacle.

First, from the outset the government's commitment to genuine devolution as distinct from cosmetic devolution was in some doubt. For example there was little attempt to reduce government elsewhere: no commitment to reduce local government to one tier or to lower the number of Scottish MPs as Kilbrandon had recommended. Indeed on this last point John Smith, before his appointment as minister in charge of devolution, had been particularly forthright: 'Members of the party who were pressing for devolution to a Scottish government without the loss of the office of Secretary of State and a reduction in the numbers of Scottish MPs at Westminster were being dishonest' (*Scotsman*, 19 August 1974). But on taking charge he stood on his head and refused to consider such a change. The total effect was to leave the not unfair impression on the minds of the public that they were being asked to approve more and costlier government, not less, as devolution proper implies.

Second, the refusal to countenance PR was not just a rebuttal of Liberal wishes and a rejection of the Kilbrandon recommendations, but enabled influential pro-assembly people to get off the hook. One of the most significant 'reluctant no' speeches was made by Lord Home who said that better proposals including PR were required (this despite the new Tory leader's known hostility to such talk). His views carried much weight especially since the lack of PR meant the threat of one-party (Labour) control and hence the assembly dominated by the interests of the most populous region, Strathclyde, instead of being constituted with its own internal checks and balances. Indeed highly significant in the poll outcome was the discrepancy between acceptance in the central belt and rejection in the outlying areas of Scotland largely for this reason.

Third, as though these policy defects were not in themselves large-enough impediments, the government completely mishandled the referendum itself. Unlike the European precedent they decided to give no financial resources or explanatory literature to the two opposing sides. This itself militated against the high turnout required to reach the 40 per cent hurdle and discouraged the formation of effective 'umbrella' all-party organizations on each side (these had been particularly important in the European referendum). They then compounded the error by deciding to have a Labour Party 'pro' campaign in which Mr Callaghan beamed down from street posters exhorting us to say 'yes'. Doubtless this had been decided in the previous autumn when the Prime Minister's personal popularity was high (and when he should in my repeated view have called the election). But to invite the populace to say 'yes' apparently to a government which was highly unpopular and had overstayed their welcome through an appalling winter of discontent was, to put it mildly, counter-productive. The referendum campaign was a disunited and dispiriting affair turning long-standing advocates of devolution like myself into 'reluctant yes' supporters. The Tories skilfully exploited their 'no' campaign as a precursor to the general election.

The basic fault throughout was putting Labour Party considerations first and effective devolution second. John Smith, whose qualities I had known and liked since the year he was President of the Labour Club at Glasgow University and I of the Liberals at Edinburgh, certainly earned his place in the cabinet for his patient and skilful handling of the issue. To me he resembles a Scottish Roy Hattersley, and he summed up the error in the government's approach in a friendly conversation with me about PR. There was no point in discussing the intellectual or political merits of the case: the Scottish Executive of the Labour Party would not have it, and that was that.

In the end, the Labour Party proved to be the undoing of devolution, and the handling of devolution proved to be the undoing of the Labour government, for without hitherto tacit nationalist support and without the Lib–Lab pact the government inevitably fell in the vote of confidence on 28 March 1979.

Chapter 9

The Pact in Danger

The story of devolution began before the pact, continued through it and right up to the 1979 general election, but I now return to the chronological tale of the pact itself.

The winter of 1977–8 was dominated politically by speculation that though the economic situation was improving, thanks to tight control over inflation, the Lib–Lab pact might break asunder under the strain of continuing Liberal electoral failure and hence restlessness in the party. The Tory vultures were permanently waiting in the wings, with some justification, for this to happen.

Two events early in the new session highlighted the difficulty of projecting Liberal influence on the government. We had carefully timed a public rally in London to coincide with the day of the Queen's Speech at which I would make a major speech outlining our achievements in detail. I wrote up the day as follows:

> The state opening is 'blacked' by TV technicians. I write furiously my speech for the London rally that evening and get it to the press gallery before James Callaghan has spoken. It contains two references to his speech, but not a single newspaper realizes that this therefore means I had foreknowledge of it. Sometimes I think unless you spell things out in words of one syllable to the lobby they don't grasp anything.
>
> Arrive at the Conway Hall and do the *Newsday* interview in a poky room backstage with Michael Charlton using the outside broadcast unit which is to cover my speech. I'm due to speak at 7.45 but it is thought the TV technicians may 'pull the plugs out' at 8.15. Therefore we begin at 7.35 and I delete the phrase in my speech referring to the TV workers' action lest they pull out instantly. Such is their power of censorship. In any event the nine o'clock news is blacked out, so my speech was carried only by ITN and BBC2.

The following Wednesday was my chance to speak in the Commons in the general debate on the government's programme. The opening speaker for the government was to be the Secretary of State for Employment:

> Phoned Albert Booth to agree what I could say on the all-party campaign on youth unemployment to twist the Tories' tail in the Queen's Speech debate. In the event he makes such a boring and lengthy speech that by the time I follow him both the chamber and the press gallery are empty and what I say doesn't get much coverage.

So the two major occasions for trumpeting Liberal input in the government's programme were frustrated.

The next day I found myself having unintentioned difficulties with two of my colleagues. Michael Foot asked to see me and when I arrived he rather crossly brandished a photocopy of a letter from Emlyn Hooson to another member of the government saying that David Steel wanted to know how he intended to vote on PR for the European elections and that the Prime Minister had pledged his private support for PR.

> This is disastrous on two counts. (I discover later from his secretary that he has sent this letter to ten ministers.) First, it makes our canvass rather too formal and annoys the government. Second, it gives away the PM's intention which he has yet to reveal to his colleagues.
>
> I try to rescue what I can by explaining to Foot that if we don't get PR we must for the sake of the Lib–Lab agreement be able to blame the Tories. A Labour majority in favour is essential and to get that we will need a solid payroll vote. He takes the point and says that once we get past second reading and possible guillotine then there is still time to explain this to ministers, and that he and Jim may well help to do so.
>
> Emlyn next day is abashed at what he has done but I didn't tell him who had reported the letter. He assumes it to be some junior minister at Defence.
>
> No sooner is that meeting over and I return to the chamber to listen to John Pardoe in the economic debate when he turns to me: 'I have committed a terrible sin,' he says, 'I've done a Crossman.' This opens all manner of ghastly possibilities. 'You

remember he left cabinet papers at Prunier's? Well I left the notes Denis Healey sent to you on profit-sharing together with my counter-proposals in a loo in the House. They disappeared and turned up next day in a big brown envelope in the mail.' Later one of the Tory treasury spokesmen, John Nott, assures him that 'we'll not make use of them'. So they have fallen into Tory hands.

Sunday 13 November was Armistice Day, the only Sunday in the year that I spend in London.

Arrive slightly late at the old Home Office for the Cenotaph ceremony. The brass are already lined up inside with a gap between Margaret Thatcher and Ted Heath for myself. Both look relieved that I turned up and they fail to address a word to each other throughout. I make polite conversation to her. Ted Heath recalls our lunch on the same occasion a year ago and says grandly: 'I told you all this would happen.' Indeed he did forecast that Callaghan would make approaches. He suggests we 'have a bite again soon', but he is off to Israel next week, thus incidentally being absent from the difficult devolution votes.

At the coffee and drinks afterwards I ask James Callaghan if I can talk shop for two minutes. He is talking to the Secretary of State for Defence, Fred Mulley, who inquires politely if he should withdraw. I indicate it is not necessary and he looks positively pleased. I ask JC about reaction to the press stories and the Nats' demands for votes of confidence. He and I agree they can't be confidence votes or we wouldn't get the Tories and possibly not the Nats, but there would be a general election if they lost. (He can't be serious on that.) Although *he* can't say it we agree *I* should say why they can't be confidence votes, and I then leave to write my piece for tomorrow's *Times* along these lines. Audrey Callaghan and Polly Elwyn-Jones both warmly solicitous of the family.

Evening dinner at the Italian Embassy to meet Cardinal Hume. I sit next to him over port and he tells me his grandfather went to school in Kelso. He knows the Borders well from his holidays there. A warm man. Sir John Hunt, Secretary to the Cabinet, is there (his wife is Hume's sister), and gratuitously opens up on the Lib–Lab agreement saying that in his view it is working remarkably well considering how few resources there are to underpin it.

Roy Hattersley puts in a plug again for upward promotion in the legislative queue of his Bill on competition policy and consumer protection. I told him I had mentioned it to the PM before. He indicates that he had gathered from reports of our exchange that neither of us really had understood what it was all about. I concede this to be true and he laughs and says we must both try harder.

That week I also carried out my promise to the Prime Minister to lobby the TUC direct on the merits of profit-sharing:

Bleary eyed after 2am vote on Wales, went to see Len Murray this morning at Congress House at 9.30am to discuss profit-sharing. He took my straight political point about restraining trade-union reaction to the government's paper to unenthusiasm rather than hostility since this was the one distinctly Liberal thing we had got out of the Lib–Lab agreement.

He would like trade-union machinery involved in setting up profit-sharing schemes. I said this could well happen in some companies but he could hardly expect it in the legislation. He accepted that.

He also thought, which surprised me, that it would be useful to set the proposals in the wider general context of industrial democracy and that it would be better if the profit-sharing paper followed close behind the industrial democracy paper being prepared by Shirley Williams's committee.

All the time I was aware of the mounting pressure within the party to secure the PR vote in the European election Bill as the paramount issue. That weekend I was due in Brussels where I concentrated on that issue:

Left for Brussels where the weekend was usefully spent. Friday lunched with Roy Jenkins who agreed to raise the European PR issue with Mrs Thatcher when she visits in a fortnight. I spoke both at the European Liberal and Democratic Congress and at the press conference afterwards. They adopted a declaration drafted by me calling for Britain to adopt PR for Europe. Had useful chat with the German Liberal leader (and Foreign Secretary) Hans--Dietrich Genscher and Prime

Minister Gaston Thorn of Luxembourg and new German Economics Minister Otto Lambsdorff.

The following week there was another bad by-election result for us in Bournemouth. It came through on the Friday when I was touring the north-west. On visits to Liverpool, Manchester and Rochdale I had to put up with angry demonstrations by striking firemen and their wives against the 10 per cent pay policy. One such looked a bit nasty and I was hustled out of a building with a cordon of police, but I couldn't help reflecting that it must be a long time since the leader of the Liberal Party was demonstrated against because of the government's policy! But the retinue of press and television cameras and reporters were more interested in the poor Liberal showing at Bournemouth, where our vote was about halved.

As bad luck would have it, the party council was meeting that Saturday in Derby while I was on tour elsewhere. They were in understandably depressed and worried mood and passed a resolution demanding a special assembly if Labour failed to deliver PR for Europe:

> This council, acting under clause G2 of the constitution resolves that:
>
> (a) if the House of Commons fails to pass the Regional List System for direct elections to Europe as a result of the failure of a substantial majority of Labour MPs to support it, a special meeting of the Assembly shall be summoned;
>
> (b) the President of the Party, the Chairman of the Party and the Chairman of the Assembly Committee, acting together are here empowered to decide whether the situation defined in clause (a) has arisen, and, as appropriate, decide a time and place for a special assembly and make all the necessary arrangements;
>
> (c) the business of this meeting of the Assembly shall be to:
>
> (i) consider the future of the Lib–Lab agreement;
>
> (ii) consider and decide upon the attitude of the Liberal Party to any direct elections Bill held under an undemocratic voting system;
>
> (iii) consider such questions of political and electoral strategy that the standing committee may put before it.

I had already made it known that this issue could and should not be the breaking point of the Lib–Lab agreement and that if it were,

I would resign, but *The Observer* on Sunday led with a much stronger version, namely that I would resign if an assembly were even held. Adam Raphael and Michael Nally wrote: 'Mr David Steel is to warn colleagues that he will resign as Liberal Leader if the party insists on holding a special conference to decide whether to pull out of the pact with the Government.' Much as I detested the thought of a special assembly I could hardly prevent it taking place or adopt such a high-handed attitude. But *The Observer* was right to see the approach of a storm.

Monday 28 November 1977

Saw JC at Number Ten for nearly an hour, over two cups of tea. We discussed the firemen's strike and I asked him if he was certain to hold the 10 per cent line. He said he wanted my view. They were likely to ask to come and see him (Len Murray had tipped him off). Indeed while we were talking a phone message came through from Terry Parry the general secretary of the FBU (Fire Brigades Union) and we broke off for a couple of minutes while he pondered on when best to see them – 9am tomorrow he decided.

He could either (a) say he hadn't properly appreciated their case and give in substantially, (b) say 10 per cent was the limit, or (c) look for 10 per cent plus fringes which would not too openly get round the limit. We both agreed (b) was the best course and I told him of the firemen's demonstrations and the meeting with my local firemen that morning.

We discussed the working of the pay policy generally and he seemed to think it was working well with only minor breaches in the private sector.

He told me he had accepted my nomination of two senior Councillors, Stanley Rundle of Richmond and Aubrey Herbert of Suffolk, for the New Year's Honours list, and he now thought he would have his life peerage list in the spring.

On devolution I suggested it would be best not to have the referendum before the general election, but perhaps in November after one. He repeated that contrary to newspaper speculation 'neither you nor I' are thinking of a spring election. I drew his attention to the possibility of including a second question on independence if the referendum had to be held before an election as a way of spiking the Nats' guns.

Turning to Europe he told me of his battle that morning with the NEC of the Labour Party on the issue. He told them that they wouldn't be sitting round the table with the Cabinet (as they were) but for the Lib-Lab pact and that he would be supporting PR. Telling the NEC he added was the equivalent of a public announcement! This is very helpful.

I told him we intended to lobby hard especially on ministers, and that his clear support was therefore welcome. He said that it was the universal Labour view that direct elections should not be held before a general election. I said I didn't mind so long as they were not delayed beyond November 1978 since otherwise other European countries would find excuses about 1979. He thought not and that May–June 1979 would be okay. I said it was vital to get the vote on the election system in the House out of the way before any hint of date slippage, otherwise we would lose the squeeze on the Tories. He said I should talk to M. Foot on that but he entirely took the point.

He asked what I was going to do about the party council resolution. (I suggested that his party and mine might have a special joint conference on the issue while we took a weekend off, which appealed to him greatly.)

I said that I proposed firstly to secure a majority of Labour MPs, second if that failed to fend off a special assembly until the House of Lords had a chance to refer it back, and third if faced with an assembly to win the argument or else resign. He said 'for heaven's sake don't do that' and asked who would take over if I did. I said possibly Pardoe but as he and most of the MPs were supporting my line it was difficult to say. He said that it was all very well his threatening to go at his age, but not me at mine. [He had in fact done so to the Labour Party executive.] I said I wan't threatening, but that I could not lead the party if it refused to follow the direction I sought. In that event it would be better for the party to get a new leader.

We went downstairs to look at the tapes. As he expected the NEC account was there. I introduced him to Archy Kirkwood. As we left by the cabinet office door (where we entered) Andrew Gifford was waiting outside the front door with the car and a phone call was made to bring him round. The Somali Vice-President was arriving and Number Ten didn't want me mixed up in the photographs. As he didn't show up AK and I walked round to find two policemen peering into the engine. The starter had jammed. I drove while AG, AK and a policeman pushed the car down Downing Street to start. Just as well there were no photographers around.

Monday 5–Wednesday 7 December 1977

Various meetings with M. Foot and M. Cocks over the tactics on the PR debate on Europe, which end up with the firm agreement to go for the PR vote next Tuesday evening.

I question JC on his Wednesday statement reporting on the Council of Ministers' meeting at Brussels, having primed him via telephone message first. Both he and Owen have put maximum pressure on the Tories by repeating that elections can only be held in time if PR system adopted.

HANSARD 7 December: Col. 1391

'Mr David Steel: Can he [The Prime Minister] confirm or repudiate the suggestion that appeared in the Press that he and the Foreign Secretary appear to have abandoned all prospect of meeting the deadline on direct elections?

'The Prime Minister: No. I shall be interested to see how the voting goes when the issue comes up. If the House takes a decision before Christmas, that in itself will decide on what date the elections can be held. (Hon. Members: "Oh.") Opposition Members should not be so sensitive about this. They will have a chance of taking a decision, although I am not sure that they are so keen about taking a decision now that we are coming up to it.'

Emlyn and I have two meetings with Merlyn Rees on the firemen's strike. The 10 per cent line is being held by the government.

Thursday 8 December 1977

I see JC in his room at the House and thank him for all the help being given on the PR vote and explain growing pressure in the party. I stress the need to press on with the profit-sharing paper. Since it has been delayed because of our extra input there should be a written question and answer explaining this.

He tells me about forthcoming increases in nationalized industry board salaries, and milk. I can see the relevance of neither.

Evidence that pressure was actively being put on backbenchers came on Sunday after a live TV interview from Edinburgh:

With Brian Walden on *Weekend World* live from Edinburgh. Afterwards entertaining lunch at John Mackintosh's when he tells us how he was approached by Michael Cocks on the PR vote and told of the need to keep David Steel happy. He had replied that it was one of his chief objects in life and therefore he would co-operate.

Monday 12 December 1977

Dublin, to deliver the Luthuli Memorial Lecture at Trinity College. Dinner beforehand with Michael O'Kennedy the Irish Foreign Minister who confirms that at the Council of Ministers the week before Callaghan and Owen had played the direct elections issue absolutely straight indicating that it would be entirely up to the House of Commons to determine the method and hence date of election, but that he thought it unlikely the House would back PR.

O'Kennedy (and various Irish TV and newspaper reporters) are much exercised over PR for the three seats in Northern Ireland. They believe the United Ulster Unionist Coalition (UUUC) and the Tories may combine to prevent it. They are also worried by persistent rumours that there is a secret deal between the UUUC and the Labour government to keep the latter in office, and that this is affecting Northern Ireland policy. Callaghan had told Lynch that this was nonsense, and I said I thought so too. No doubt the Speaker's Conference on extra Northern Ireland seats would keep the UUUC happier and Powell is bitterly anti-Tory, but that doesn't amount to a deal.

Tuesday 13 December 1977

Fateful day of the direct elections debate. Jeremy makes a good speech and Heath a bad one in favour of PR. The Scotnats decide to abstain which lowers our expected vote by eleven. We lose by eighty-seven. The Tories' three-line whipped 'free' vote does the trick with a huge anti-PR vote on their side.

Immediately after the vote the MPs gather in the whip's office, much angrier and upset than I had expected. Benn, Shore, Orme and Booth had voted against and this particularly upset them. Callaghan rings three times asking to see me, but I say he must wait until I have finished discussion with my colleagues. Just before 11 I go round to see him in his room. He is, unusually, alone and says he wanted to tell me the Labour figures – 146 for, 115 against PR.

I say that is much as I expected, but warn him that my colleagues are very upset and that we will definitely be unable to fend off the special assembly. I tell him we have agreed to meet in the morning and I hope they'll feel calmer after sleep, and that I'll let him know the outcome. We leave rather sorrowfully.

Wednesday 14 December 1977

The *Daily Mail* publishes an entirely fictional account of my meeting with JC on the front page:

A stormy meeting between Mr Callaghan and Mr Steel early today looked like the beginning of the end of the Lib-Lab pact ... he [Steel] marched round to confront Mr Callaghan with the question: What went wrong with your vote? Mr Callaghan was already angry.... According to Liberal MPs the meeting was terse and sharp. Mr Steel made it clear that there was no longer a majority of his parliamentary party in favour of continuing the pact. Mr Callaghan was equally abrasive. He insisted that the Liberals should sort themselves out and decide what they wanted to do. Then he is reported to have challenged Mr Steel: 'If you are going to break it off, you had better give me a firm date. I don't want it to go straggling on....'

I cancel all my engagements including a visit from the Israeli ambassador. After a sleepless night I am not in a very good mood or very clear headed to chair the meeting which begins at 10am. I play for time and agree to discuss the position with the PM in the afternoon. We issue a statement saying that the vote indicated that the Parliamentary Labour Party deliberately sought to destroy the Lib–Lab agreement.

In the early afternoon D. Ginsburg, a Labour backbencher, came to see me to suggest we try a second vote at report stage to see whether more Labour MPs and Tories will come to their senses. I say the idea is worth considering and ask Michael

Cocks to come to see me. He also thinks it might be a possible course and I say I'll see how the PM reacts.

John Pardoe had also been in to see me and was generally fed up; the pay policy was not working, Healey's figures were wrong, and Healey had fobbed him off with a meeting on the subject after Christmas. This is alarming and I ring Healey at the Treasury who insists that his figures are not wrong. Earnings increases are running at 12–14 per cent, not the 17 per cent claimed by Pardoe, and we are well on course on the inflation figures and will continue to be with the tax reduction in the budget. He also says that if Pardoe presses for an earlier meeting of course he can have one – he just thought it more useful to await the local authority settlements. I arrange for Healey and Pardoe to meet next week.

Then I ask Jo to see me because he was absent from the morning meeting but is going on *Nationwide*. He thinks the party is making a fuss about the PR vote, that this is not the issue to break the pact. Alan Beith and I persuade him to come and say so to the resumed party meeting at 6pm.

As Jo says in his *Memoirs*:

'When the List system for European elections was rejected in the Commons, it came as no surprise to me. I did not see that it altered our situation. A meeting of the Parliamentary Party was called on the evening of the defeat for the next morning. As I already had an engagement that morning and did not see that anything unexpected, or indeed damaging, had occurred, I did not attend. I was only told of it late the night before. That afternoon I was astonished to hear that with the Party in a mood of near panic Steel had gone to see Callaghan apparently to protest against a breach of their agreement. Callaghan had honoured his undertaking and said so.'

At 4pm JC comes over from Downing Street to see me. Ken Stowe is away and Philip Wood is standing in. Michael Foot is also there and JC asks if I mind that. I say I welcome it, tell him I have no suggestions to make and that I have just bought time by coming to see him, but that the parliamentary party is in uncertain mood. I raise the suggestion of the report stage tactic without enthusiasm but ask if he has any ideas on what we might do.

He has been ruffled by some of the lunchtime remarks of colleagues, especially Smith and Pardoe. He starts referring to the written text of our July letters and says they've adhered totally to the agreement and that while the free vote was a free vote people like Michael had fallen over backwards to help. They should not be abused now. I tell him there is no need for him to tell me all this, because I agree and had spent the morning telling my colleagues that. He says he wants to set it on the record, nodding in the direction of the scribbling Wood.

Then he says he doesn't like the report stage idea and that the Libs must just make up their minds whether they are going on. Is there anything he can do to help? I say I doubt it, but tell him of our concern on pay policy, taxation and profit-sharing, and disagreement on defence cuts. But I tell him there is nothing new in all this and don't see the point in discussing it. He agrees.

He asks who is being difficult and advises that I should 'watch Pardoe' who has been saying things in the city. (I check with John later and this appears to be a reference to his telephone calls to city experts advising both him and the government.) JC adds entertainingly that 'after all Michael spends all his time trying to knife me'. Foot grins: 'Yes, but my aim is not very good.' I point out that JP has told me openly of his anxieties about the effectiveness of government policy. I tell him I'm going back to my colleagues to have another try. He asks me to come back and tell him if it is all off. I say I will do so either way around 7.30pm.

6pm we meet in Room J again. This time I tell the MPs firmly that my view is we should press on with the agreement and fight for it in the assembly unless they wish to break it off and fight the next election on a different strategy and with a different leader. Jo says his piece. The argument rages for nearly an hour and a half. Cyril presses a proposal to break off. I ask for a straw poll. This resulted in four showing hands to break off, six for going on, two abstained and one was absent. The pact remained intact on the most tenuous basis.

7.30pm I go to see JC. He is surprised and relieved at the turn of events. I tell him I can't see us going on beyond July and we may have to take it in two stages – 1. to the budget,

2. to July with the Finance Bill if the tax and profit-sharing proposals are okay. There is also the problem of the special assembly. He repeats his warning about Pardoe whom he continues to misunderstand and mistrust. He asks if he can do anything to help. I ask him to jack up his ministers in their relationships with the Libs. I tell him of the Healey conversation (but he knows already!) and complain about Benn not consulting on his conservation measures. He is surprised and annoyed to hear this and makes a note. I also suggest I have a hand in preparing the preface of the green paper on profit-sharing.

He asks what I propose to do and I repeat that if the assembly doesn't back the agreement I will resign. I tell him that there is always the Scottish Assembly. At this point he asks Wood to leave us. He says that whatever happens I must come and talk to him about my future. I tell him I intend to stay if I can and as we go to the door he says he has valued 'our friendship' and we shake hands and wish each other a happy Christmas. He thinks things may settle down in the party over Christmas, and I say I hope he is right.

I do BBC and ITN news interviews and then go with Archy, Andrew and Clement Freud to a splendidly relaxed dinner at the Clermont Club.

Thursday 15 December 1977

Another fairly sleepless night. The press reaction is predictable. Filthy reports in the *Mail* and *Express*, but good editorials in the *Guardian* and *Times*.

I decide to write a long letter to the candidates. Beith persuades me to take out the direct 'resignation' paragraph, but I tell him that is my intention if things go the wrong way at the special assembly. I take it back home for Judy to read and we revise it late at night after the kids' school concert.

In my letter to candidates, I put my position forthrightly as follows:

No one can say that they did not know where I stood, and *I* am not going to change course now. I think *the Party* would be crazy to change course, but you are entitled to do so if you wish at the Special Assembly. This is a democratic party. I have explained to the Prime Minister that while he, the Leader of a large party and head of the Government may justifiably ignore or defy a conference decision, such as the one made by the Labour Conference rejecting direct elections themselves, the Liberal Party is not in the same position. A small group of 13, especially if divided among themselves, cannot go against the decision of our Assembly on its entire strategy and keep the Liberal Party intact. Therefore if you decide to break off the Agreement it will be broken.

I could not be party to breaking the Agreement delivered over my signature to the Prime Minister. You did not conclude it: I did, and therefore you may not have the same inhibition. Nor could I lead the party into an election arguing a case in which I do not believe. No party can put its leader in that position.

I want to be able to argue the case for a better way of running Britain and illustrate it as we've never been able to before by pointing to a successful period of political co-operation. I cannot do that if various organs of the party have periodic hysterics over some aspect of the Agreement. Nor can we thereby expect to portray ourselves as reliable and constructive partners if we secure the balance of power. No, the whole strategy would be in tatters and unsaleable. The party must therefore make up its mind calmly but firmly on what course it wants to take.

Monday 19 December 1977

To London to face four anti-pact Liberals on *Panorama*. All flights cancelled because of fog at Gatwick and Heathrow. We hire a Piper Aztec and suffer a noisy and cramped two-hour journey to Luton and then travel in a decrepit local taxi getting lost in the fog on the M1. I arrive in not very good shape for the broadcast, but it goes off passably well.

About this time the party mandarins decided that the special assembly would be held on 21 January and searched around for a suitable venue. One suggestion was Belle Vue Zoo, Manchester. Although it was patiently explained to me that it was not actually in the zoo itself but a conference hall on the complex, I was by now so irritable on the whole subject of the special assembly that I said bluntly that this would make a laughing stock of the whole exercise and if they chose to go there I would not attend. My office did a pacifying job between me and those involved and it was fixed for Blackpool. Jo Grimond consoled me with the entertaining view that on the contrary Belle Vue Zoo was an entirely appropriate place for such an event, and my mind went back to conversations with him before I became leader when he asked me to stop and ponder seriously whether the Liberal Party was capable of becoming an effective political instrument.

Tuesday 20 December 1977

Meeting of the Privy Council at the palace to swear in Prince Charles as a member of the council. Donald Stewart, leader of the Scottish National Party, asks for a lift and we arrive far too early and therefore sit in the courtyard while an ambassador arrives with three horse-drawn carriages to present credentials. Meantime I ascertain that if there were a vote of confidence the SNP are all over the place. Donald thinks they should support the government till the devolution Bill is through, but he says his hawks think they should go for an early election. On defence they might abstain. We agree that we ought to keep in touch in the event of a 'hung parliament' at the next election.

Inside, while waiting for the royals, Margaret Thatcher arrives and greets me with forced icy charm. Later Prince Philip draws both of us into conversation and then walks off landing me with her again. We exchange meaningless pleasantries about the Christmas recess.

A very quick ceremony. Michael Foot as Lord President departs to fetch Charles on the command of the Queen. The rest of us form a line – the Lord Chancellor, Archbishop of Canterbury, and a clutch of the cabinet. Charles walks in, shakes hands with his mother who says she is so pleased he is now a member of the council. He walks down the line shaking hands with each of us (which he has already done outside informally) and that's it. No kneeling, no oath. All over in two minutes. He says afterwards that he doesn't take the oath because he is assumed to be loyal anyway.

It is incredible that all these busy people have to turn up for this fairly meaningless gesture. The Queen says 'That's all the business of the council?' Michael nods and Prince Philip says 'except for the business next door' and leads the rush to the drinks trays.

I tell Charles that I am the only one who is not all that pleased that he is now a PC and he says right away 'why, because you were the youngest? But you're not much older than me!'

In the afternoon, after a late Christmas lunch with all the office, a long meeting with Michael Foot. I stress the need to get the green paper on profit-sharing published by 21 January when the special assembly is to meet. He agrees this is important but did not think it would be ready. He would chase it up. He also agreed to bring forward the Home Loans Bill before 21 January. We discussed possible subjects of votes of confidence like defence or others like devaluation of the green pound which could be awkward and we agreed the need for careful advance planning on these.

On the European Bill they had not yet decided whether to try for a guillotine. If they didn't get it he thinks it best to abandon the Bill rather than have it take up parliamentary time to no purpose. He agrees that constituency schedule amendments should be resisted by the government.

He expresses concern about the assembly on 21 January even asking questions which I can't answer about who all goes to it.

Later a meeting with John Pardoe subsequently joined by Alan Beith and Richard Wainwright. I am relieved that JP and RW appear to have simmered down and are willing to accept that the agreement can go on till July with me giving notice in June of its ending. AB and RW go off with Archy to the standing committee with an acceptable draft resolution for the assembly and I go to the Rowntree Trust party with Andrew and Ann. Later some of us adjourn to the Outer Circle Policy Unit where Mark Bonham Carter presides over a magnificent buffet. Archy and Evelyn Hill arrive from the standing committee which only by eight votes to six stopped a 'break the pact now' resolution going forward.

Archy Kirkwood, Pratap Chitnis and myself retire to another room with General Election Committee chairman, Gruff Evans, to mull over the state of the party. Then Archy and I catch the night sleeper.

Wednesday 21 December 1977
Arrive at Edinburgh and go to airport to collect my car which we left there. It has been giving a lot of trouble with over-

heating. Get as far as Rossleigh's garage at Corstorphine where it again boils. They are full of gloom and amazed that it has done 47,000 miles without major engine trouble. I decide I cannot spend a fortune putting it right and still be nervous about its unreliability. So I say a sad farewell to my beautiful Stag and buy a second-hand Rover on the spot. I can't afford it, but the new model I looked at was £6,000. A slightly depressing start to the Christmas recess!

Christmas Eve

Phone calls from:

1. Emlyn Hooson, who has been contacted by Carolyn Morrison with a view to discussions on defence cuts. This clearly stems from my last talk with Foot. He wants to know if he can take a public stance. I say he should, and he is expecting a detailed brief from Mulley. There is likely to be a 'two-year' defence white paper with an increase in expenditure in the second year.

2. Michael Foot who says that 21 January looks an impossible deadline for publication of the green paper on profit-sharing, but I should be able to see the final text by then and we can agree what I should say to the special conference. He wishes me a happy Christmas, but still sounds concerned about the outcome of 21 January.

3. John Pardoe who reports on appallingly mutually aggressive meeting on pay policy on Wednesday between himself and Healey, who had insulted him in front of three officials. JP very amazed and gave as good as he got. Clearly John has upset not only the PM but Healey as well. John says he will send me a full note. He still sounds very gloomy and unsettled. He called Healey on the radio 'the second worst Chancellor since the war'.

Christmas recess

Spent a long time pondering and on the telephone to various colleagues. The more I think about it the more unacceptable is the 'July deadline' solution proposed in the Standing Committee's option. I write to RW who is holidaying in Portugal to say so. Apart from JP who has come round, JT, EH and DP all fall back into line with various degrees of enthusiasm.

Tuesday 3 January 1978

Evans and Tordoff spend all morning at Ettrick Bridge and stay for lunch. I make clear the unacceptability of the proposed options and together we hammer out a draft compromise which allows the assembly to hope the thing will be over by July but allows it to *continue* until such time as we decide. This gets a lot of coverage next day and an ITN crew pursues me in Andrew Haddon's farmyard.

Saturday 7 January 1978

Richard Holme, one of my regular advisers, joins us in Ettrick Bridge and I begin the first of four drafts for the party broadcast.

Tuesday 10 January 1978

I attend the Standing Committee and put my case. They agree to recommend to the assembly that there be a vote on my option only versus ending now. This is a major step forward.

Thursday 12 January 1978

The broadcast goes out and is well received. Also gets a good press Friday am.

Wednesday 11 January 1978

A wretched day spent recording the party political broadcast amid all the doubts of a BBC industrial dispute. At one point we were told we could not record and Peter Hardiman Scott is sent down by the Director-General as we lunch and wait. Eventually the go-ahead is given and we agree on the third 'take'. Still doubts about editing and transmission.

A subdued parliamentary party meeting at which in Cyril's absence they agree to back my line without dissent.

Friday 13 January 1978

An appalling meeting with the LPO Executive which at one point is a shouting match. Several say the party is disintegrating, and I listen to worthy verbal essays about 'participating democracy' etc. Towards the end one member actually mentioned inflation. I leave angry and depressed for a quick curry with Evans, Tordoff and party president Michael Steed before Archy and I join the night train.

Saturday 14 January 1978

A splendid Scottish Liberal conference in Glasgow restores my morale with a 210–12 vote in favour of continuing the pact. The Welsh Party Council also backs continuing the agreement.

Monday 16 January 1978

I take the day off and go riding with Judy.

Wednesday 18 January &
Thursday 19 January 1978

The consultative committee meets and considers the green pound question. They reach agreement (see Appendix 8) on an agreed amendment to the Tory motion establishing virtually a 10 per cent devaluation in two stages. This to be tabled in our joint names.

Friday 20 January 1978

Friday morning's *Express* carries a front-page lead story by Chapman Pincher about my leaking budget secrets. The whole thing is so ludicrous that no one pays any attention.

However, the PM has vetoed the agreed Commons motion on the green pound wanting to leave out one phrase. Foot asks to see me and John Silkin talks on the phone. To both I make it clear that they must deal with Howells and Pardoe.

AK, AG and I drive to Blackpool leaving this unresolved. JC is on a train to Cardiff, and the amendment has to be down by 4pm. When we reach Blackpool I am told no agreement was reached and the government put down their own version in their own name. Late at night an even more ludicrous *Express* front page for Saturday is relayed, headed 'Der Pact' and misquoting me concerning earlier talks with Genscher, giving the impression that the Germans were responsible for the pact. All this because I told Pincher that I thought the Schmidt/Genscher coalition success may have had some influence on Callaghan's thinking.

This is very worrying, in the midst of talks with Cyril and Gruff Evans. I emphasize to Cyril the need to keep the party in one piece and suggest he makes a second speech (after the vote) of a conciliatory nature. I talk to John Pardoe on the phone after 1am to get the green pound negotiations clear.

Saturday 21 January 1978

In the morning I see the papers and am horrified by the Pincher story. The only thing to do is to ridicule it and I decide to add to my speech. I phone Tom McCaffrey who confirms Number Ten taking the same line. The Opera House is full and the debate goes very well. I dodge all the formalities of calling on the mayor and after being photographed barefoot in the suite go to the hall. A break for a filthy picnic lunch in a backstage dressing-room during which Judy and Graeme arrive.

A very good debate, but I am nervous partly because too much of my speech is off the cuff and I take notes throughout. The whole thing ends well and Cyril makes his unity plea very effectively.

I drive back to Ettrick Bridge with Judy, totally exhausted and stopping for a Kentucky Fried Chicken to eat on the road out of Blackpool. Home just in time to see good reports on the ten o'clock bulletins.

The special assembly resolution said:

> This assembly recognises that the agreement between the Liberal MPs and the Labour government has been in the national interest because it has strengthened the economy at a time of grave danger, has ensured that the government maintains the attack on inflation, and has changed the direction of what had previously been a doctrinaire socialist government; deplores the fact that many Labour MPs have undermined this constructive approach to the country's problems, for example by co-operating with the Conservative leadership to frustrate democratic reform and European ideals;
> expects by the time the Finance Bill 1978 is enacted the Lib–Lab parliamentary agreement will have successfully achieved its immediate purpose for the good of the country;
> and believes that the agreement should continue only until, in the light of this resolution, the leader of the party, in consultation with the senior officers of the party, and with the parliamentary party, decides to end it;
> and is determined that, thereafter, the Liberal Party shall seek the endorsement of the British people, at a general election, for its achievements and policies.

In retrospect I was wrong to be so hostile to the holding of a special assembly. There was a genuine and high quality debate which was well received by the media. The party left with higher morale, and I was able to make a most forceful speech from the rostrum challenging the 'what's in it for us?' approach of the opponents rather than the traditional reading of a prepared text from the platform. It all greatly helped to shape the party into a more responsible and cohesive mould and was contrary to all my forebodings. The total effect was strengthening to the unity of the parliamentary party and to the Lib–Lab agreement itself. The vote for the resolution had gone 1,727 to 520. Peter Jenkins in *The Guardian* began his piece: 'Mr Steel is armed with a mandate to do virtually what he likes' – a pardonably euphoric exaggeration.

Chapter 10

The 1978 Budget and the Life of the Pact Draws Quietly to its Close

On Monday 23 January, after the weekend endorsement of the pact by the Liberal Party, it was back to business as usual:

> Overnight train to London and speak at Granada TV lunch, presenting *What the Papers Say* awards. When I get back I receive the expected summons to see Foot. He congratulated me on the assembly result. I tell him I've done enough to keep the Lib–Lab pact on the rails over the last few weeks and don't intend to do it on each individual issue. The consultative committee must be made to work.
>
> The government loses its agriculture motion by ten votes and has to accept the $7\frac{1}{2}$ per cent green pound devaluation. It could have avoided this humiliation by sticking to what had been agreed in the consultative committee.

> *Tuesday 24 January 1978*
>
> Overnight great attempts by the government, because of the larger devaluation forced on them, to blame Tories and Libs for higher food prices. I reply to this on the Jimmy Young radio programme and at a speech to the newspaper conference.

> *Wednesday 25 January 1978*
>
> Dinner at Number Ten for Greek PM Karamanlis. I discover that the Greek Liberals (Centre Democratic Union) having done badly at the last election (down from forty-two seats to fifteen) had their elderly leader resign. They are busy changing the rules to allow more than MPs to vote for a new leader and are then having a leadership election and a special assembly to do this and discuss strategy. An astonishing parallel.
>
> Among those present is Moss Evans, the new TGWU boss, who is a cheerful Welshman. We chat for a bit. Both David Owen and Fred Mulley are effusive about Blackpool. As is

Lord Robens. JC asks after dinner how I am feeling post-Blackpool and we engage in some small talk, before I return to the House for the committee stage of the Scotland Bill.

Wednesday 1 February 1978

JC comes up to me in the division lobby and says: 'I see you're deserting me these days.'

I say: 'What do you mean? I'm here voting with you.'

'Yes,' he replies, 'but you haven't been to see me for ages.'

'You ought to be pleased about that,' I retort, 'it means things are going well.'

'You haven't told me about Blackpool.'

'No,' I reply, 'but I assume you read the papers.'

'Ah well,' he says, 'it just goes to show that what our parties need is firmness – it always pays.'

After a bit more banter of this kind we have some words on Thatcher's appalling utterances on immigration on which he is grateful for our support.

Monday 6 February 1978

M. Foot asks to see me about the Electricity and Nuclear Materials Bill. He has heard from Tony Benn about our anxieties. I outline four areas of concern and ask for a brief on these points. I also tell him that since Benn has been bloody about the whole Lib–Lab agreement he can hardly expect enthusiastic co-operation. I urge him not to put it into the consultative committee until I have talked to the PM next day.

Tuesday 7 February 1978

A forty-five-minute meeting after questions with the PM. I outline my concern about the Bill and about a recent speech by Benn. He says we shouldn't read these texts too closely, but I have the Transport House text of Benn's speech with me and point out he contradicts what the PM and Healey have both said about the role of the Liberals in economic recovery. Also I remind JC about his view that the only legislation to come forward should have sex appeal. I suggest this electricity re-organization has none. It is mainly a centralization measure giving yet more powers to Benn himself.

He is surprised to learn it runs to fifty clauses and I suggest the Bill on school governors instead. He says he would like the Bill to set up a Co-operative Development Agency, and I agree that would be preferable.

He says that a statement on reducing the size of the steel industry (followed by a Bill) will have to be made by Easter. I told him of the talk between RW, myself and Villiers and he reckons we have to face a smaller steel industry because the steel industry throughout Europe will take another eight years to pick up. He talks about the effect in Cardiff and other measures that will be needed.

We discuss the forthcoming white paper on the use of North Sea oil revenues.

He says he is having trouble with the TUC on industrial democracy and may have to settle for a government white paper, though he would like legislation in 1978-9.

He asks about our attitude on defence. I tell him all seems now well, following the new defence white paper increasing necessary expenditure, and Mulley's briefings of Libs, of which he has details in front of him.

We turn to the economy. He says the January retail price index (RPI) is excellent and will be published in ten days, and the forecast for February is good. He is worried about our lack of sales of gilts at which point I am lost, but he thinks euphoria misplaced. Housebuilding is coming up which is a good sign. I suggest that our budget tax reform proposals should be taken seriously.

He asks about the pre-Christmas Healey/Pardoe row on which he has received a written account – 'the meeting ended abruptly'. I said I had a similar account but suggest we do nothing about it.

He asks how we'll do in the Ilford by-election, and I tell him badly, but we won't fight Garscadden.

I tell him I'd like to discuss the political outlook in more detail around Easter. He says he won't be willing to decide on an October election till July, but he sees my need to have a period of independence. He asks if I see Thatcher at all, and I tell him I don't. He says he wants to play the next election as the leader of a left-wing party heading towards the centre, while she is the leader of a right-wing party heading towards the right. He says he needs a good size Liberal vote, and that the next parliament may well be hung. Mischievously he asks what will I say to Mrs T. if she has a small lead? I tell him that is a recurring nightmare and he laughs and says he will do his best to relieve me of it.

We also discussed the timing of the devolution referendums. He asked again if I thought it best to have them before or after an election. I said after.

Monday 13 February 1978

Foot discusses the Electricity Bill and says the government now feels committed to it. We agree that the consultative committee should therefore meet tomorrow to discuss this.

Tuesday 14 February 1978

At question time the PM suddenly suggests a three-party meeting to discuss race relations and immigration. This is the first I (and obviously Mrs T.) had heard of it. Immediately afterwards I was due to give a lobby briefing and therefore announced my readiness to participate. I was asked whether I had been consulted and said that I had not.

As soon as I returned to my room there was a message to see JC right away. He said he proposed writing to Mrs T. and myself to follow up the suggestion and wanted my approval of the draft, which was being typed. When it came, I made a couple of minor alterations which were agreed (see Appendix 9). He asked whether I thought it likely she would accept and I said I thought it unlikely. (Later in the day she issued a statement stalling.)

While waiting for the letter we discussed our invitation to him to dine with us in one of the Commons rooms. He had declined, but thought it best to invite the Liberal MPs to meet him. We discuss the pros and cons of the House v. Number Ten, tea v. no tea and announcement v. no announcement.

The consultative committee meets in the evening with Tony Benn included and fails to reach agreement on the Electricity Bill (see Appendix 10).

Sunday 19 February 1978

The meeting at the National Liberal Club (NLC) of the MPs, party officers, standing committee and general election committee. A useful paper on election strategy by Michael Steed.

By the end of the evening with only one minor tiff between myself and a couple of more difficult people, the meeting with remarkable acquiescence adopts a document setting out our strategic aim for the next election of securing the balance of power, and expressing readiness to work with either party after the next election. Truly Blackpool has seen a catharsis. It has taken nearly four years to get them this far.

Monday 20 February 1978

Another meeting of the consultative committee at which Penhaligon is handed a copy of the draft Electricity Bill in the hope of persuading us to accept it. We will discuss it on Wednesday at the party meeting.

Wednesday 22 February 1978

A meeting in the morning with JP to discuss our strategy for the joint meeting with Healey and Barnett. JP has not met Healey since their pre-Christmas row, and he seems slightly apprehensive. (Talking in the lobby to Joel Barnett the night before he said to me 'I think you and I may have to hold the coats.')

3pm we go across to the Treasury and stay for an hour and a quarter. Healey says he will meet us specifically on three points in the budget: profit-sharing, changes in agricultural assessment to average income over two years, and increased tax allowances on hotel construction or extension. I point out that this will hardly be sufficient and that if he expects our support in the Finance Bill there must be at least a move towards our tax proposals. He agrees that support for the Finance Bill is crucial and says there may be an election if he can't carry the budget. I point out that this perturbs us not, but that we too would like agreement if possible. He undertakes, after much protest, to discuss with the CBI etc. our proposal to raise a surcharge on employers' national insurance.

On petrol we tell him bluntly that we won't agree to an increase until Hattersley's department sorts out the policy of the oil companies in charging more in rural areas. We agree cigarettes could go up, but he is reluctant to increase beer in election year (also it's gone up already). At a later point he says he never spends more than 3 per cent of his time thinking about politics. I say 'oh come off it' and he cheerfully gives me two fingers across the table. The whole atmosphere is very different from the last Healey/Pardoe confrontation. We leave with JP determined to lobby the various employer organizations in support of our policy to reduce the higher rates of income tax by accepting a higher national insurance surcharge. (On child benefit we are met with technical objections to our proposals to speed up the increase in payments.)

That evening there is yet another consultative committee on the Electricity Bill at which we finally give a definite 'no' to Benn's proposals. This fact is beginning to leak out anyway via the government.

Thursday 23 February 1978

At business questions M. Foot admits we are the obstacle to the Electricity Bill but says he is still hopeful of persuading us. The subject is raised at the Parliamentary Labour Party and in the government's lobby briefing.

In the evening dinner at the French ambassador's house. I sit next to Harold Lever's attractive wife who assures me that he is very grateful to us for putting him on to small businesses which he is enjoying. Over drinks beforehand Lever says he hopes to do more in relieving them of form-filling. Sir John Hunt nods agreement.

After dinner I get into a corner with the ambassador, David Basnett, Denis Healey and Freddie Fisher, the editor of the *Financial Times*. Part of the discussion passes me by as it centres on international finance. Healey says I should use my influence on Lambsdorff, the new German Economics Minister (FDP), but I point out that I have only met him once and omit to add that I hadn't realized what he was talking about anyway. We get on to the more familiar ground about the next pay policy round and I applaud Basnett's recent article on incomes policy.

At one point the conversation turns to the prospects in the French election and then to ours. General condemnation of Mrs T. on immigration and other matters.

At about 11.30 I ask Healey if he will give me a lift back to the House on his way to Number Eleven. I want to pick up my cases and tidy up before going for the night train home. This gives me the chance of a quarter of an hour alone with him, which he seizes. 'What are the chances of your backing the Finance Bill,' he asks. I make it clear that he really must shift on the balance of taxes question. If he does I tell him I think we will be all right. He again undertakes to discuss this seriously with the CBI, etc. He also complains that JP is liable to leak. I say this is not so and that he and I are both very aware of the need to preserve budget confidentiality.

I phone JP next day to tell him of this exchange so that he takes it seriously.

Monday 6 March 1978

Meeting with Foot at his request to discuss:

1. Direct elections Bill in Lords. We agree there should be a free vote on PR.

2. Steel industry. He wants Liberal co-operation on drafting amendment to Tory motion for debate on Thursday. I agree we should try, and refer him to RW.

3. Electricity Bill. He noted my observations at the weekend about Benn but responded jovially over a cup of tea. Nevertheless he said they wanted the Bill. I told him I would see the electricity chairman Frank Tombs and union leader Frank Chapple. Also we would prepare a list of detailed objections to the Bill, of which I have just seen the draft.

Tuesday 7 March 1978

A long meeting with JC.

I begin on the budget and stress our argument for a surcharge on the employers' national insurance as the method of paying for reductions in the higher rates of income tax. I don't think he was aware of the political arguments for this till now and he took note without promising anything other than a talk with Healey. We agreed that support for the Finance Bill was crucial both from us and his own backbenchers.

I said how much we welcomed the success of all Lever's supra-departmental activities on small businesses but suggested he should have a mini-department of his own to institutionalize this work, with perhaps an official from each department concerned. JC not keen on this and thought Lever best left on his own.

He asked about our attitude to the steel industry. I quizzed him on reduction and he said it would have to come down from 42 million liquid tons per annum to around 20–22 million tons with a corresponding loss of employment. He showed me the draft government amendment but I said Varley and Wainwright were dealing with it. Varley will produce a detailed statement before Easter with a two- to three-year programme of cuts. He said previous loss figures were wrong because they were based on over-optimistic world-wide forecasts, but there was no attempt to deceive.

He raised the matter of the Electricity Bill and said it was badly needed. It was not 'Bennery' as I had described at the weekend but a cabinet decision. I cited some specific objections and he said these were details. But I said we had to reach agreement on the measure. He said Penhaligon was being obstructive but I said *our* decision was collective too. I told him I would see Tombs and Chapple and he emphasized the need for speed. I said it would be helpful to get Tory support for second reading.

Finally, we discussed the ending of the agreement in July. He said he might wish to put a package for 1978–9 to me and get a straight yes or no on support, but generally he seemed to favour an October election. I asked if he was as gloomy as portrayed. He said not, but that Audrey had been unwell, having picked up a bug in India. Also over the last three weeks he had developed a deep contempt for Mrs T. on immigration. I said I shared that. He asked me to see him more regularly.

Monday 20 March 1978

Saw JC for an hour. He came over specially from Number Ten and I said I could just as easily have gone over to see him.

He said that Varley would be revealing all the troubles of the steel industry in a statement on Wednesday, and there would be no need for a temporary additional help for British Leyland. He also gave me a copy of tomorrow's white paper on North Sea oil.

We went on to discuss the budget. I began by saying that we were trying to reach agreement with Healey so that we could support the detailed passage of the Finance Bill. Since this would involve voting against attractive amendments tabled by the Tories in election year, this was asking a lot of us. Our hand would have to be seen in the budget. In previous conversations he had accepted the need for us to retrieve our slipped Tory votes. The best way to help us do that was to see that the reductions in income tax in the middle and upper levels were carried out at our behest.

I said we were agreed on the priority for raised thresholds and for a lower rate band. He said the latter may be politically necessary to give to the TUC since they were going to be offended by other parts of the budget, and I accepted that. I said that I did not see how there would be room in addition for lowering the burden at higher levels unless he raised revenue elsewhere. I accepted that he would be unwilling to raise VAT to 10 per cent or impose other duties because of the effect on the retail price index. I suggested cigarettes could be a special exemption on health grounds.

I went into detail on the argument for $1\frac{1}{2}$ per cent or 1 per cent increase on the employers' national insurance as raising a further £1,155 million and he seemed to accept the argument. It could not begin till August, and the feed through the RPI would be only half a per cent in a full year.

After our discussion on the budget JC asked Ken Stowe to leave us for a 'political discussion'.

We went on to discuss election dates. He still wants the option of going on to 1979. He doesn't think inflation will necessarily go back to double figures as some forecast, and that in any case people will feel better off over a longer period. There is also the possibility of favourable action from the July economic world summit which could help another budget before the election. He agrees an election desirable after the devolution Bills are on the statute book but before referendums, which I argue points to October. He is against the suggestion of my 'giving notice' in April.

Tuesday 21 March 1978

A long morning meeting with Healey and Joel Barnett, JP and self, and two Treasury officials going over our budget proposals. I focus on the political argument as I had done with JC and we then descend into detailed arithmetic. They appear willing to grant our arguments in principle but not in any particular. John and I agree to refer the matter again to the party meeting for a final decision on our sticking points.

At one point Healey says across the table: 'I suppose you think we're heartless bastards.'

'Oh no, Denis,' I responded, 'not heartless.'

The civil servants laughed and Healey gave a v-sign across the table. All very amicable but not very constructive.

Wednesday 22 March 1978

Albert Booth turns up in my office to discuss his Dock Work Order. He comes armed with a sheaf of papers. I told him firmly I was sticking to Nancy Seear's objections to extending union power in his scheme, but if he cared to have the documents photocopied for her I would see she considered them. Meantime our objections stood.

Monday 3 April 1978

My plane from Edinburgh was nearly two hours late and as a result a pre-arranged meeting in the afternoon at the Treasury had to be put off till after 7pm. This was the second session with JP and myself across the table from Healey and Barnett (with Healey's political adviser and a Treasury official taking notes).

It lasted only forty-five minutes and although we rattled through a series of apparently agreed minor measures, it became obvious early on that we had made little or no progress on increasing indirect taxes in order to finance greater reductions in income tax. They seemed narked by the publicity and favourable comment Pardoe's proposals had received. Indeed the conversation turned quickly to the need for a summer election were the government defeated on financial measures. At one stage Healey and Pardoe were locked in the old argument about petrol tax, and the temperature was noticeably rising. I said that it seemed likely that we would support the budget strategy but press on amendments during the committee stage of the Finance Bill. I said I personally liked summer elections, which was obviously not the reaction they were either wanting or expecting.

JP said afterwards that if I had not been present there would have been another row. I went straight back with him to dinner at his house. Next morning we were astonished to read on the front pages of *The Times* and *The Guardian* an obviously

Healey-inspired version of our meeting, based on his warning us of an early election.

Wednesday 5 April 1978

We launch our tax proposal document at a press conference in the NLC with radio and TV interviews. It is all well reported and reasonably well received.

In the evening after a meeting with Dr Waldheim, United Nations Secretary-General, I saw Michael Foot in his room to discuss the political implications of the budget. We had a cordial meeting with him offering me a whisky 'before you lot put it up!' He shares my view that it would be madness to go to the country before the end of the session and throw away all the legislation on devolution, etc., which is still in the pipeline. I repeated that if Healey did not go far enough on income tax we must be free to push him further.

Merlyn Rees also asked to see me, and as I bumped into him in the corridor he came into my room. I offered him a drink which he accepted gratefully as he was suffering from jet lag after returning from the States. He plans to announce a rebuttal of the Select Committee on race relations and immigration tomorrow along with the ten-year statistics.

Thursday 6 April 1978

Leslie Murphy, the chairman of the NEB [National Enterprise Board], rang very worried about Monday's vote to provide extra cash for Leyland and NEB. He had discussions with RW on Leyland but not much on NEB, which the Tories were likely to oppose, and he wanted to make himself available for further consultation. RW was on a train to Leeds, but I rang him in the evening and he said he would be in touch with Murphy before Monday.

Monday 10 April 1978

Saw Healey at his request *à deux* on Privy Council terms in his rooms in the Commons. Took Graeme to get his autograph. He outlined most of the budget proposals which had been given to the cabinet that morning. I told him I was delighted with the full range of proposals on small businesses and on profit-sharing, but not happy on income tax. He said that he would indicate our joint acceptance in principle both of the payroll tax and widening the new lower rate band in future years. He also said he would standardize VAT at 10 per cent at the earliest (post-election?) opportunity, but he would not say so publicly.

I got the distinct impression that he had been defeated in cabinet on reducing the higher rate band because he dropped a heavy hint that he would not mind being defeated on that during the Finance Bill. Clearly for Labour to propose this is politically difficult, but to accept defeat on it relatively easy.

Later in the afternoon a meeting with JC. I told him that subject to what my colleagues said I thought we would be able to support the budget in principle but move amendments in the committee. He talked about his private meetings at the weekend with Giscard and Schmidt and went on about the international financial scene at which my eyes glazed over.

I asked him to reconsider carefully the Lords' vote in favour of PR for Scotland, but not to give me an answer right away as it would be the wrong one! He said that if there were any evidence of a shift in opinion on the issue he would consider it.

I asked about the civil list. He said there would be a 9 per cent increase for the Royal Family, though what the individual allocation would be was a matter for the Queen.

Tuesday 25 April 1978

After a good deal of huffing and puffing over budget differences in the press over the weekend, JP had seen Joel Barnett last night, and I arranged to see him to find out how he got on after I returned from a by-election meeting at Epsom. He was in a difficult mood. Barnett had yielded nothing and even suggested that the phrase in my July letter about the transfer of taxation had not been agreed by the PM. I said that was nonsense and I would pursue that argument with the PM next day. JP is particularly sore about the bad press he has had, especially in *The Guardian* that morning, which contrasted his tone with a 'sober and thoughtful' speech by me. He stayed for two hours till 12.30am in troubled mood.

Wednesday 26 April 1978

Meeting with JC just after noon, a meeting which he desperately did not want to be 'at his request'. I told Ken Stowe none of our meetings were ever at either's request and that's how it should remain.

He is worried about effects on the markets of 'knocking holes' in the budget by Commons votes. Public spending for April is already excessive and will cause upset. The reserves could drop. The markets already uncertain partly because of Denis and Joel's silly nonsense over a possible July budget.

I raised Barnett's theory about the July letters. JC says Barnett has 'no authority' to put such an interpretation on what he and I had drafted. He then went through the July letter admitting the failure to switch taxation but claiming good marks on all the other points. He asks if JP rocking the boat. I told him not so. JP representing our collective view, although he is a mercurial character. I said 'you have some too' which he admits. 'You and I will just have to keep calm. I will have to play the Finance Bill day by day.' I agree that is only sensible course, and tell him we will announce our income tax amendments that evening. He reads a minute from the Department of Health and Social Security saying that the national insurance surcharge cannot be introduced in October–November for administrative reasons (when I tell him this later JP is surprised that they have gone into such detail). JC says that if it would help I can bring JP along for a general political chat.

He is worried about the cost on the public sector borrowing requirement of our proposals, and I repeat that he must just take the Bill day by day because the prospect of all opposition parties agreeing on all proposals is remote.

He says that after Thatcher's intervention yesterday supporting a breach of pay guidelines on services pay he has a growing contempt for her, which he has indicated before. He also says there could be a minority Labour government after the next election, which is why he agrees the present pact should not end in a row, but as I've said in an orderly way at the end of July.

He then looks at the year's by-election results and tries to persuade me that the Tories have not even reached their February 1974 peak. I don't know whether he believes this, or is just whistling to keep his or my spirits up. It doesn't look that way to me. I remind him that if our vote continues to collapse this will help the Tories.

Tuesday 9 May 1978

Saw JC for about twenty minutes to seek his reaction to my suggestion of announcing before the Liberal Party Council due at the end of next week in Peterborough that the Lib–Lab pact would definitely end in July. His reaction was as he put it one of 'consternation'. It would upset the markets further. Things were not all as bad as they looked, and all advice he was getting was to go on to 1979. He would prefer that we waited till July.

Enough upsets already after last night's defeat on one penny off standard rate. He was gloomy about the prospects of further defeats on Wednesday on the Finance Bill.

I spent much of the day with RJ trying to stop our candidate at the Hamilton by-election from going ahead, because we had totally inadequate strength on the ground and would get a very bloody nose.

In the evening JP suggests we try JC on either PR for Scotland or a referendum on PR for Westminster.

A second meeting with JC to which I took JP. Michael Foot was present at my suggestion. I said I wanted to consider how best we ended the Lib–Lab agreement and pointed to a difficult Party Council coming up on Saturday the 19th. I said I wanted to know his reaction to the suggestion that prior to that we should exchange letters bringing the agreement to an end at the end of July. His reply was 'total consternation'.

Markets already unsettled because of last night's defeat on the Finance Bill (one penny off income tax). Spent approx. $150 million that morning bolstering the pound.

He suggested wait till Whitsun recess to make announcement. I said that my view was that unless PR for Scotland (following Lords' vote) or referendum on PR for Westminster (which JP backed strongly) was proposed we would not be able to consider continuing agreement in 1978–9 and therefore there should be a general election in the autumn. He said he thought we might consider Queen's Speech on its merits, but I said I thought this course undesirable.

We agreed the government should have a fortnight to consider the PR point.

We also discussed today's forthcoming debates on higher income tax changes and he questioned Pardoe's arithmetic on cost. JP said figures came from Treasury, but apart from one vote raising threshold from £7,000 to £8,000 government should be safe in divisions 'provided all your ministers are awake' (a reference to Judith Hart's having slept through a vote the night before). JC replied, 'We are not in the Chamber now Mr Pardoe', but in good humour. I promised to let them know later how we were voting on each amendment.

JC said on leaving: 'You and I would have sorted these differences out' and he is clearly annoyed that Healey and Pardoe had not reached agreement.

JP commented afterwards on how the atmosphere was different from his meetings at the Treasury.

Tuesday 16 May 1978

CBI dinner. JC speaking as guest of honour. Long and amicable discussion with Merlyn Rees who is my neighbour.

Sir John Methven tells me before dinner that he saw Healey on Tuesday the 9th after one penny vote and he was in very bad mood. He said next time CBI would walk out. Healey complained that they had told Pardoe they would accept national insurance surcharge but had not told him. Methven said he had never asked.

Lift back from Merlyn Rees. As we arrived dinner-jacketed back at the H of C Peter Shore and Stan Orme greet us with the words '*Some* of us have been sustaining the Labour government.' A vote ten minutes later. JC is in a lounge suit after his speech at the dinner. I tackled him in the lobby: 'That was a remarkably quick change.' He has the grace to look slightly embarrassed.

Tuesday 23 May 1978

Attended United Newspapers lunch at the Savoy. At Lord Barnetson's table apart from myself were Ted Heath, Harold Wilson, Denis Healey and the Archbishop of Canterbury – a very strange mixture. I had the misfortune to sit next to Harold

Wilson who was a crashing bore and talked about nothing else except his chairmanship of the city inquiry. He has a theory that the real power in the land are the pension funds, not the Chancellor of the Exchequer. 'You, Denis, don't know what's going on.'

This did not endear him to Healey who replied: 'I remember what you said, Harold, I know what's going on; I'm going on.'

'Yes,' said Harold, '4 May 1969.'

Afterwards Healey gave me a lift back in his official car and remarked on how extraordinary it was that Harold could remember such bits of useless information. He also said: 'I suppose you're going to pull out in July.' I said it looked like it and it was increasingly difficult to delay a definite announcement. The Party Council had been expecting it on Saturday, and my routine speech to them had been rather flatly received as a result.

Wednesday 24 May 1978

At three o'clock I took JP to see the PM and Michael Foot. JC began by saying that they had considered our two proposals on PR but there was no go. We said we had not expected otherwise, and that we should discuss the timing and manner of ending the agreement.

To my surprise JC then referred to my conversation with Healey the previous day and asked if the Party Council had been difficult. I explained that the parliamentary party as well as the party outside were now waiting for a definite ending announcement.

JC said he would prefer no announcement till the end of July but saw our difficulties. He was to be in the States next week (the Whitsun recess) which we had had in mind and would prefer to be here when the deed was done. Could we postpone it till the week after? I felt we were in danger of being strung along. Now was never the right moment, and JC admitted he would like to play for time.

I said in any case I wanted to make the announcement *before* the Hamilton by-election next Wednesday because we were bound to do disastrously and I didn't want to appear to be taking the step in its aftermath; therefore it would be better done before he went, possibly on Friday. I could come back from Holyrood and the General Assembly of the Church of Scotland.

He was against an exchange of letters and thought I had better make a unilateral statement. I said I would show a draft to him and we would think further on precise timing. He asked about the parliamentary party and I said they would have to be informed.

He said, turning to Foot, that next time they would have to involve their parliamentary party apparently. (A reference to my *World this Weekend* interview.) I laughed and asked what made him think it was him we would be talking to. He smiled and said to us, 'I can't quite imagine you crawling into bed with Margaret Thatcher.'

Later that afternoon I drafted a statement and showed it to John and Alan. We sent it across to Number Ten and I reported vaguely to the parliamentary meeting at 6pm on the state of play. Later in the evening I agreed a couple of minor altera-tions on the telephone. Friday seemed unattractive from a publicity viewpoint and we agreed on tomorrow at 3.30 after PM's questions. He would tell the cabinet in the morning.

I had to excuse myself from going to Holyrood in the after-noon, fix TV interviews and a lobby briefing and fly to Edin-burgh for the evening. Ken Stowe said to tell the Lord High Willie Ross that the PM was sure he would understand. The PM was now intending to issue a statement in reply which he would let me see after approval by cabinet.

Thursday 25 May 1978

Most of the MPs were telephoned or seen during the morning and early afternoon. There were no leaks, but in the middle of the cabinet Ken Stowe phoned to say the Chancellor pleaded for delay by an hour or hour and a half until the Stock Exchange closed. He and the Governor of the Bank of England were mak-ing announcements at lunchtime on minimum lending rate, PSBR limits and other topics which were unsettling enough. The PM requested my agreement. So we rejigged for 4.30 which left me very tight for interviewing and the lobby before flying north.

We made it. Callaghan's statement arrived at lunchtime and

was generous. Lead story on all news bulletins and next day's papers.

After dinner at Holyrood I did a good live interview down the line with Robin Day.

'...I AM PLEASED TO THINK THAT I SHALL BE ABLE TO FREE SOCIETY FROM ANY FURTHER EFFECTS OF HIS PRESENCE THOUGH I FEAR THAT IT IS AT A COST WHICH WILL GIVE PAIN TO MY FRIENDS AND ESPECIALLY MY DEAR WATSON, TO YOU. I HAVE ALREADY EXPLAINED TO YOU, HOWEVER, THAT MY CAREER HAD IN ANY CASE REACHED ITS CRISIS, AND THAT NO POSSIBLE CONCLUSION TO IT COULD BE MORE CONGENIAL TO ME THAN THIS...'

(Sherlock Holmes last letter to Dr Watson - 'THE FINAL PROBLEM')

Tuesday 6 June 1978

Lunch at Danish Embassy to meet Poul Hartling the former Liberal Prime Minister of Denmark, now UN High Commissioner for Refugees. He and his London representative both tell me of their bad impression of Mrs T. after a meeting that morning. John Davies, Tory Shadow Foreign Secretary, had tried to minimize the damage, but she had left them with the impression of being insufficiently sympathetic to the world refugee problem, and lumped them in with immigration generally.

Wednesday 7 June 1978

Morning meeting with Morarji Desai, PM of India, which also followed one he had had with Mrs T. He too does not disguise his dislike of her narrowness and says he thinks they must be very unsure of themselves to become so strident. When he talked of her proposed referendum on capital punishment I said I hoped he would not take offence if I suggested that their next manifesto pledge might be to take back India. He enjoyed the joke.

In the afternoon Harold Lever suddenly asks to see me and comes to my room. The cabinet would decide tomorrow to recoup the budget votes by introducing the national insurance surcharge (NIS). The PM had asked him to come and tell me and he had replied: 'I would rather have done so at the beginning.' I indicated my annoyance that this had not indeed been done as an agreed measure and complained that Healey had badly mishandled the thing politically. I told Lever he could tell Healey that, and that I had myself tried to persuade him to take this step quite apart from our official negotiations. Lever said he would convey my reaction and that I was not able to promise Liberal support for the measure, though I expected we would back it.

I asked how much, and he had to telephone Healey's office to recall – 2½ per cent which will raise £490 million this year, and £1,600 million in a full year.

In the evening dinner at Claridge's given by the Indian PM. Various members of the cabinet present. JC sees M. Foot and myself talking beforehand and comes over to ask: 'You two agreed on everything then?' I replied that I now understood changes would be announced after cabinet tomorrow and that I wanted to know if I could consult my colleagues, especially JP. JC said he would prefer not, muttered about action on the gilt-edged markets and said Pardoe was a leaker. (Lever had mentioned earlier he was speaking to me on Privy Council terms.) I said I thought Denis had been very stubborn and at that point JC said he didn't agree but was dragged away to sign an agreement with Desai. He left cheerily saying 'I'm relying on you', meaning they still wished me to make a statement supporting the NIS.

After dinner I got a lift back from Michael Foot and repeated my complaint about the way Healey had handled things. He said Healey could not have got agreement from the Labour Party for the higher rate of income tax cuts. I said he could have blamed us and got away with it, but he hadn't even tried. I reminded him of the occasion I had come to see him to avert the Healey–Pardoe conflict and the subsequent government defeat. He said he would arrange for someone to tell us the exact timing tomorrow.

When I got back to the House I saw JP and decided to tell him the NIS proposal and was relieved to find him sharing my astonishment and bewilderment as to what we should do. Finally he said: 'It's a political decision, not an economic one and I leave it to you.'

Thursday 8 June 1978

Ken Stowe phones in the middle of cabinet to confirm decisions taken and timing 12.30pm. He repeats PM requests my support. I read him draft statement (agreed by JP) of acceptance and my scorning of Healey at which he laughs and says I wouldn't expect him to comment on that part.

Then Harold Lever phones to tell me the same thing, which is a little surprising, and I tell him that, while accepting the proposal, I will attack Healey. He says: 'Much as I love Denis I think it was a terrible blunder.'

Tuesday 13 June 1978

A very difficult meeting of the MPs in my room at 3.30pm. They feel strongly against the 2½ per cent NIS and at the lack of consultation. Half want to abstain on the Healey censure vote and half to vote against. CS and RW feel particularly strongly against, with CS saying he will vote that way regardless.

I telephone K. Stowe and put him in the picture, and at about 6pm I leave with Judy and carrying my kilt outfit to go and change for the state banquet at Buck House. On the way out I bump into Merlyn Rees clutching a pair of braces and muttering about having to change into white tie.

When we get to the Palace there is a short queue at the top of the stairs waiting to be presented. By sheer chance Denis and Edna Healey come up immediately behind and he says 'watch it' in a cheery way. We exchange pleasantries.

After a fairly boring dinner we all withdraw to a drawing room for coffee, and I talk with the young Duchess of Gloucester, Princess Margaret and Princess Alexandra. In the midst of this and in full view of various ministers and diplomats, Healey comes up and takes me to one side. We chat for about ten minutes and I tell him of our difficulties and repeat my censure of the way he handled the negotiations leading to this state of affairs. We discuss the possibility of making tomorrow's vote one of confidence.

After some talk with other people including Len Murray, we leave just at the same time as the PM and MF who are off to meet and discuss what to do. I repeat that the vote of confidence is a possibility but suggest he sees JP in the morning and that Harold Lever should see RW.

After midnight I phone both JP and AB to put them in the picture.

Wednesday 14 June 1978

At 9am I meet AB and JP in my room and we have a gloomy discussion before JP goes off to see Healey. He returns as does RW who was summoned by Lever in his pyjamas. Lever seems to have spent most of his time disagreeing with Healey which was not helpful. Neither JP nor RW feels we are any nearer a solution. Just before 11am I was invited round to Number Ten where I see JC and MF in the cabinet room. I stay for a quarter of an hour.

He has rejected my idea of reducing NIS to $1\frac{1}{2}$ per cent and says they cannot let the Chancellor go, and that subject to what we may say he will with great reluctance announce a vote of confidence and if defeated go to the palace and have an election which neither of us wants. He says this sorrowfully and claims 'there is no law against slitting our own throats'.

He is bedevilled by President Ceausescu of Romania for five hours on his state visit but will await our reaction.

Our party meeting at 12.45 is more subdued. They agree (CS reserving) to abstain if vote of confidence, otherwise to vote against, but willing to vote in favour if reduced to $1\frac{1}{2}$ per cent.

Just as I am through to Number Ten to convey this at about 1.20pm the PM comes on the line and I tell him direct. He says he is keeping Ceausescu waiting for lunch but wants to tell me that he therefore thinks it best to announce a vote of confidence. M. Foot will chair a cabinet meeting at 2pm and I arrange to see him immediately to tell him our views. This I do at 1.30 and he says he'll let me know the outcome of the cabinet meeting.

At 3pm they announce that it will be a vote of confidence. Geoffrey Howe opens in strident form abusing both Healey and ourselves. Healey replies very effectively full of self-justification. I have little prepared and dread making a speech in these circumstances, but the barracking is not too bad, and neither is the speech which I keep brief. I don't announce our voting intentions just in case the arithmetic calls for a last-minute alteration.

Jim Prior winds up in a rambling ineffective speech leaving the PM an easy wind-up. During the evening Gwynfor Evans tells me his three are abstaining, so the government is safe if we abstain. Cyril is still difficult until he interrupts the PM near the end to ask if he will discuss the $2\frac{1}{2}$ per cent with us. Then I pass him a note on the bench and he agrees to abstain as well. Afterwards I discover he got wind of separate plans by Clement Freud and Geraint Howells to vote *for* the government if he voted against thus cancelling the effect of his vote!

I do a bad interview with David Holmes for BBC news and a better one with David Rose for ITN.

Next day: Predictable rage from the Tories and the Tory press at the government's survival.

Tuesday 20 June 1978

I phoned K. Stowe at Number Ten to say that it might be useful to meet the PM after questions as I was preparing a speech for the Scottish Liberal Party conference and would be calling for an October election. If he had any objection I would wish to discuss. The reply came back that he quite understood and I should just go ahead.

Friday 23 June 1978

A thin turnout at the SLP conference with the papers full of recrimination on Hamilton result, where we failed to reach even 1,000 votes. I deliver my speech, do half a dozen radio and TV interviews and leave Perth in haste. Speech well covered in the media that night and next day.

Tuesday 27 June 1978

Message from Number Ten asking me and JP to meet PM, Healey, Foot and Barnett on Wednesday at 3pm. Puzzled by this as I had not asked for a meeting. JC is in America for two days and so is Ken Stowe. I talk to John Medway at Number Ten after it is confirmed that the meeting is at PM's request to discuss $2\frac{1}{2}$ per cent NI surcharge. I say that this is surely incorrect and that Healey and Pardoe should discuss first. He says he'll check with Stowe. Later he rings back, Stowe having consulted PM and PM having talked to Healey on the phone from New York to say that PM requests meeting because the issue is not a Treasury one but Prime Ministerial one.

Wednesday 28 June 1978

The Guardian carries story in advance of today's meeting by Ian Aitken which upsets both Number Ten and ourselves.

Liberals say they are not obliged to side with Government

PM SEES STEEL OVER TAX VOTE

The Prime Minister has called in Mr David Steel and his senior colleagues in the Liberal Party for talks today about the looming confrontation between the Government and the Liberals over the proposal by the Chancellor to increase the surcharge on National Insurance contributions.

When JP and I go round to JC's room I take a note reminding

me of how we got to this pass in the first place, ready to blame Healey again. (Barnett left just before meeting.)

JC very welcoming and asks me to confirm pact still in being till end of July. I do so, and he says 'then you and I must discuss the £440 m. hole in the budget – the others can just listen'. He asked if we would consider supporting $2\frac{1}{2}$ per cent to recoup the full £440 m. gap and I said we would go no further than $1\frac{1}{2}$ per cent. He said, 'I don't suppose we deal in quarters!'

He said the smaller £140 m. gap would therefore remain. I said I had marvelled at my moderation in not blaming Healey more during the debate, but that was a problem of his creation. If need be we would consider tobacco.

He then asked about dividend control. They had word of companies about to declare enormous dividends when controls ended in July and would we support legislation?

Healey joined in discussion prefacing his remarks with: 'May I speak Jim?' and I asked Pardoe to reply. He said provided it were part of tough pay policy of course we would support such legislation.

'NEW BALLS, PLEASE!'

Discussion drifted on to pay and John resurrected his old idea of pay policy linked to NI penalty surcharge, which would get over all problems of $1\frac{1}{2}$ per cent or $2\frac{1}{2}$ per cent. Healey doesn't quite grasp the proposal and he and Pardoe meet afterwards to discuss it further.

John and I report to party meeting. They accept $1\frac{1}{2}$ per cent and I do lobby briefing as does Number Ten with satisfactory headlines next day.

At 10pm I saw Michael Foot and Michael Cocks re the guillotine on Lords' amendments to the Scotland Bill. I had seen Donald Stewart earlier and he confirmed all Nats would be voting for it. Therefore our bargaining position was weak. But it was agreed there should be a rerun of the PR debate

'Waiter, there's a fly in my soup.' 'Quite disgusting, sir, but we'd be in the soup without him.'

without John Smith making his 'anti' speech again, and with a more genuine free vote: i.e. less payroll whipped against.

Monday 10 July 1978

Talked to David Owen about the possibility of my going to Rhodesia if Tories following John Davies's visit come out with a partial Muzorewa/Smith line. He was favourably disposed provided I did not go under provisional government auspices. The invitation had come from Muzorewa.

Ken Stowe told me on the phone he had put my inquiry to the PM who took the same view and suggested if I were going I should also see Nkomo and Kaunda in Lusaka. I said I was not committed to going till I saw the Tory reaction and whether we had a spare week with the House not sitting at the beginning of August.

(In fact the Tory line was not too aggressive and the House sat into August. I postponed the visit to January 1979.)

Tuesday 11 July 1978

Healey looks in unannounced to my room and asks to come and see me later in the week to discuss pay policy and sound our views on dividend control.

Wednesday 19 July 1978

Just before party meeting JT rings to say libellous article in *Private Eye* and he is off to consult lawyers. I see a copy and it is quite dreadful.

Party meeting decides to back 'guideline' dividend policy but to oppose statutory control.

About 9pm I see the PM to tell him this. He says the cabinet may press ahead with a Bill anyway and say to the TUC in September: 'We tried but we need a Labour majority.' I say I understand that but a government defeat at this stage could be damaging and is best avoided. Also I do not want to end the session with a disagreement. He notes both points but says inclination still to proceed. He agrees with my description of it as a 'cosmetic' as far as pay policy is concerned, to appease the unions, and really not economically justified.

He then sends the civil servant (Philip Wood) out and says he wants to talk politics. What was my reaction to the Penistone by-election? I say cheerful because it indicates our vote may hold in our own seats. He agrees. Thinks next election will be 'close run'.

He says my 'even-handed' approach is dangerous and I accept that, but I think in first instance inevitable. He raises FDP comparison and I say we could alter during campaign if Thatcher shut the door. (The FDP in Germany campaign for coalition stating their partnership intentions.)

We discuss post-election situation if no overall majority. He would not wish to do a Heath and hang on to Number Ten if Tories were larger party.

I ask if we can meet in September before our conference for another political chat, especially on timing of election, and he agrees.

Monday 24 July 1978

Government lost dock labour scheme by ten votes. We voted against as promised.

Wednesday 2 August 1978

Surprising speculation in the papers over my September meeting with PM which I mentioned in answer to a question at a lobby meeting yesterday. There appears to be no other political news and therefore undue importance is attached to this.

A long talk with the Speaker in the morning at his request. A general chit-chat including what may happen to JT.

Sam Silkin, the Attorney General, telephones to say arrests will take place on Friday and their solicitors will be notified tomorrow.

Friday 4 August 1978

JT rings first thing in the morning to tell me what I already knew. Eric Avebury is with him and will provide bail.

Saturday 5–Tuesday 8 August 1978

Endless phone calls with JT and AB; JP and CF trying in vain to get coherent statement from him. JP goes to lunch with him on Sunday in Devon.

Wednesday 9 August 1978

Having dictated a suggested statement yesterday to JT's secretary he rings this morning to say he is 'appalled and aghast' at its terms, even though they were approved warmly by Eric Avebury. It turns out that this was for the benefit of his constituency chairman standing beside him. For the first time I get rather annoyed especially by this tone and tell him I shall get AB to issue a statement making it clear that we have advised him but the decision is his. He agrees that he should not come to the assembly, but I don't know if he'll even stick to that.

Wednesday 6 September 1978

Word reached me that the Prime Minister had booked a slot for a ministerial broadcast next day following a cabinet meeting in the morning. I had been doing my expected pre-election rounds of the rural areas in my constituency and made some hasty rearrangements for next day. The cabinet were all filmed and photographed emerging from Number Ten in the middle of the day, tight-lipped. The BBC and ITV arrived at my house in Ettrick Bridge ready to record my reaction to the PM's expected announcement of the election that evening. I was telephoned at lunchtime by Michael Foot who said JC had asked him to warn me in confidence in advance that far from making an election announcement he would be indicating his intention to press on for another session. My reaction was one of complete astonishment. I simply thanked him for the call, indicated my surprise and disagreement at the proposed line and sat down to prepare my public reaction. The waiting broadcasters outside realized I would have foreknowledge and wanted to record my reaction in advance to get the tapes back to the studios in time to broadcast in the early bulletins. In view of the surprise nature of the content I thought it best to decline.

Why he decided to broadcast at all was a mystery. Everyone was led to the wrong conclusion including his own party and indeed most of his cabinet. The TUC were also annoyed that he had successfully played their congress as a pre-election platform. I felt it was all a great mistake and said so.

On 27 September I had my last meeting with the Prime Minister:

He asks about our reaction to the election postponement and pulls my leg about my public denunciation. 'I didn't know you were so keen to commit suicide!' – but he thinks he can get by in the new parliament. He asks about our vote on the

Queen's Speech and says he notes I've committed myself. I point out that I left a slight loophole, to which he says, 'That's right – you should never close your options in advance', but I point out that it is not a loophole I wish to use or am likely to be able to.

If they get by on the Queen's Speech we'll tackle each issue as it comes and back them, for example, on the Rhodesia sanctions order. He understands the position.

He finally postponed the election because he thought the best they could do was come back to a hung parliament. In that case the Tories would have scented blood and harried them as in 1950–1 to another election. I disagreed with him on two counts. First, I said that if Mrs T. did not win outright their morale and unity would be destroyed. Second, unlike 1950, we now had accepted that parliament could work and with the Lib–Lab pact government be effective in a hung Commons. He still thought it best to postpone and had told the cabinet if they then lost they could lead him to the abattoir and slit his throat. He wonders if the Tories will in fact be hysterical in the new session. He has decided to have only the formal one-day spill-over to avoid any threat of a no confidence motion from the Tories.

In my reaction to the postponement of the election I said:

If, as Liberals have argued, there were ever an argument for a fixed term of parliament and removing this decision from the individual hands of the Prime Minister, this is it.

As it is, the government expects to stagger on through a difficult winter with no majority in the Commons. This will not inspire confidence.

The country had expected an election and will be disappointed. The sooner the government goes to the country the better. We shall act accordingly.

This proved wholly correct. The pay policy did not hold. There was a winter of industrial unrest, and without the pact the government lost confidence in the House culminating in their Commons defeat on 28 March 1979. Labour lost support steadily in the polls and went down to defeat in the general election.

Chapter 11

Lessons of the Lib–Lab Period

'If you knew then what you know now, would you still have done it?' The question in some such form keeps being thrown at me and my answer is an unreserved 'yes', although there are several lessons to be learned from the experience.

Yes, because the pact achieved its main short-term objective of controlling inflation, even though by cruder methods than we advocated. Looking back on how inflation started rocketing in the Barber boom of 1973 and continued upwards under Labour from 1974 to 1977, it was undeniably the only successful counter-inflation period of government. In that eighteen months the running rate of inflation came down from touching 20 per cent to under 9 per cent. It started upwards again during the last months of Labour-only government and has escalated back to 19 per cent in the first year of the new Conservative government. Mortgage holders saw their interest rates fall from $12\frac{1}{4}$ per cent to $8\frac{1}{2}$ per cent during the Lib–Lab period only to see them go up to 15 per cent since.

Yes, because it provided a much-needed parliamentary stability, though, as I shall argue in a moment, Labour could have made it more stable by using the Lib–Lab machinery more effectively to prevent defeats in the House. I'm under no illusion also that we were useful to the government in persuading the unions to accept some government policies which the government wanted anyway and which otherwise it might have had difficulty in getting accepted. Our mere existence in the vital parliamentary arithmetic was what mattered, not the weight of intellectual expertise we may have thought at times we were generously making available to the government.

Yes, because it demonstrated that bi-party government meant the extreme dogmas of the larger party were under control. There could be no further nationalization. As I've recounted, bits of state control legislation beloved by the left had to be dropped and those which were not (e.g. the dock work scheme) went down to defeat in the House. The House of Commons did enjoy a period when it actually controlled the executive. Unless the government could muster by argument a majority its measures could not pass. What Lord Hailsham has justly called 'elective dictatorship' was put in abeyance.

Yes, because it presented the country with the first taste of a distinctive Liberal policy, employee shareholding, with a tax incentive scheme which though modest in scale has already been adopted by over two hundred companies and has been more favourably received than even its authors expected.

But what about the defects? The most obvious is that the Lib–Lab agreement was cobbled together in great haste up against the deadline of a Commons vote of no confidence and with a government at the height of (deserved) mid-term unpopularity. That made it different in kind from the more durable and fundamental collaboration which could be achieved after fresh elections and with several days to pass for negotiations before the meeting of parliament.

The most obvious defect, therefore, was the one forecast by the doubters in our own ranks, namely that the failure and unpopularity of the Labour government rubbed off on us. We were lambasted for simply keeping in office a government which had outstayed its welcome. The heavy barrage of propaganda against it was something I wholly underestimated and for which I accept responsibility. It provided no atmosphere for dispassionate examination and assessment of what we were actually trying to achieve.

An element of total unfairness was added by the charge that we were 'saving our own skins' or 'scared of an election'. This was completely untrue and in our original parliamentary party meeting the general view was that we would do not too badly in an election. Subsequent events have vindicated that assessment because we entered (and survived) the 1979 election at a lower point in the polls than we were in March 1977 when we made the agreement. But however unfair, that repeated charge stuck and added to our difficulties in projecting our case positively.

A further flaw in the scheme, caused by the need for haste, was the limited consultation in both parties. It wasn't so much a Lib–Lab pact as a Steel–Callaghan pact accepted by our respective colleagues with widely varying degrees of enthusiasm or lack of it. This meant that no matter how much we wished it to succeed the pact's actual working depended on pairs of people thrown together in forced embraces from which some of them recoiled. It had its successes. Roy Hattersley and Nancy Seear lunched and conspired together to get their ingenious consumer protection and price plans higher up the Steel–Callaghan priority league. One social security minister asked me with unconcealed admiration where I had found Desmond (Lord) Banks because he knew more about the subject than he did and 'shouldn't he have been in the Commons?' To this I acidly pointed out that he was one of many who had tried and failed several times to get through our election system and so we had to put him in the Lords. But Desmond was no pushover and almost single-handedly stopped the ludicrous scheme in the pipeline to provide jobs for the trade-union boys on the boards of pension funds. Bill Rodgers as Minister of Transport admitted that David Penhaligon taught him the facts of rural transport life. Richard Wainwright with Eric Varley, and Stephen Ross with Peter Shore formed reasonable working relationships, as did Emlyn Hooson with Fred Mulley, Clement Freud with Roy Mason, and Geraint Howells with John Silkin.

But the failures were more obvious. In Cyril Smith and Albert Booth and in Tony Benn and Jo Grimond we had two pairs of people whose ideas were poles apart and who were against the pact anyway. Their partnerships were therefore not surprisingly the least productive.

The Healey–Pardoe partnership was the one with the greatest unused potential, though they achieved much. They were too alike: clever, rumbustious with a touch of arrogance, attractive personalities and quick-tempered. I suspect that John has the more original mind of the two and therein lay much of their trouble. Whatever John Pardoe's inner doubts at times on the course of events on which I had embarked no leader could have asked for a more loyal and hard-working colleague in time of trouble. Since he was my defeated opponent for the Liberal leadership both I and the party as a whole are especially grateful to him, and his loss at the general election was both a heavy political blow to the progress of the Liberal Party and a searing personal blow to me.

Neither the Prime Minister nor the Chancellor of the Exchequer placed enough reliance on him. Yet John's judgement on the economic course of events proved wholly correct. Like me he was prepared to commend to the autumn party assembly that we go on through to 1980 if need be provided 1. that the Prime Minister declared that was his intention, 2. that there was some form of wages policy that would hold to control inflation and 3. that there was some definite move on PR as I've described. Since 3. was ruled out neither of us saw any prospect of persuading the party even if 2. existed which John increasingly, and rightly, doubted. We considered that the 5 per cent incomes rule unilaterally advised by government had no chance of holding and that an October election was not only wise from the government's point of view but inevitable. How wrong we were! The Prime Minister for unaccountable reasons threw away his position of equality in the opinion polls and was forced to the country at a time when Labour was trailing well behind the Tories, thus undermining our own 'balance of power' election platform.

As I told him at our first meeting after his 'no election' broadcast, I disagreed with his analysis and his Attlee government comparison. In 1950 the Labour government was exhausted and the Tories thirsting to return to power under Churchill. They harried the government out in 1951. But if the Tories had failed to win victory in an October 1978 election the knives would have been out for their new leader and with the experience of the Lib–Lab pact behind them Labour would have found it relatively easy to form a new, possibly coalition, government if it had no overall majority but was the largest party.

That we were able to talk easily in this way gives an indication of the relationship we had built up over the period. It was an unlikely combination. I had had very few dealings with Jim Callaghan before. We were of completely different generations and backgrounds. Yet we established an easy rapport, partly because there were no leaks and we developed an early mutual trust and partly because we readily came to understand each other's limited room for manoeuvre. He had to learn, for example, that the relationship of the Liberal leader with his colleagues is wholly unlike that of the Prime Minister or Leader of the Opposition in cabinet or shadow cabinet. Apart from the few peers I selected to add to our number I had no power of hire and fire. I had to work with the eclectic selection of a dozen MPs out of the hundreds of Liberals who attempted to get elected to the Commons. All owed their positions to their own achievements and not to me.

I had to recognize his incapacity to deliver the Parliamentary Labour Party on non-Labour policy issues. This led to the crucial failure on PR for the European elections. Most of the MPS were opposed to European elections. Most were opposed to PR. To ask them to accept a combination of both was a prize piece of cheek. This was one of the fundamental weaknesses of the whole agreement, and I determined that if ever we were negotiating again after a general election with one of the major parties, the prior formal assent of that parliamentary party as a whole to any agreement would be essential.

The consultative committee was a key part of the agreement but it did not work quite as well as it should have. Since we were not in coalition it was not part of the network of cabinet machinery, and hence failure to reach agreement led to government defeats in the House as I have described on such issues as the dock work scheme, income tax levels, national insurance contributions and green pound devaluation, all of which could and should have been avoided.

The back-up facilities of the Liberal Party were pitifully small and we relied heavily on our panels of volunteer experts. A bewildering mass of important issues swam into my ken with alarming speed whenever spokesmen failed to reach agreement. I had to become an instant pontificator on all manner of hitherto unexamined topics. It was certainly no partnership between equals as the equilibrious name Lib–Lab suggested to the outside world. The Prime Minister had the whole resources of Whitehall behind him. My little office was augmented to two assistants and three secretaries.

All of which raises two questions: is a coalition preferable to such a pact? Is an electoral pact a necessary part of any such arrangement?

I take the second question first, because the answer is simpler. I can see the attractions of a temporary electoral pact, but the Prime Minister and I, though both tempted, dismissed the idea as impractical because political parties are democratic and sovereign at constituency level. The proposal has been promoted since by Austin Mitchell MP in a persuasive Fabian pamphlet. But it is open to objection on democratic principle. Why should the electors of Roxburgh, Selkirk and Peebles be denied the opportunity to vote Labour simply because the Labour candidate regularly loses his deposit? And why should Liberal voters in a Tory/Labour marginal obey the instructions of the Liberal leader on how to vote after their own candidate has been withdrawn? No: the real answer is electoral reform, not the rigging of an already unsatisfactory system. At best an electoral pact could only be a temporary expedient towards that.

The other question is more difficult. No coalition was offered in March 1977 but it would have been difficult to enter half-way through a parliament. Moreover I believe a larger number of Liberal MPs is necessary to enable an effective presence to be maintained in a coalition. The token appearance of the leader in a cabinet would not suffice. At the time of the Heath offer in 1974 the Whitehall machine produced a working blueprint for operating a coalition which is doubtless dusted down from time to time, and it reinforced my view that we would need to have a big enough pool of troops to man positions in ministries and especially key cabinet subcommittees.

Leaving aside the influence on the effectiveness of coalition government, I believe that to enter a coalition with only a dozen MPs would place an intolerable strain on the Liberal Party and especially its leader. Keeping the party in one piece was a full-time job during the pact itself without attempting to participate in running the government as well.

On the other hand there is no doubt that a full coalition would exert Liberal influence on policy and events at a crucially earlier stage, and that provided we can obtain a commitment to electoral reform the Liberal Party should be eager to operate on the inside of a future government rather than on the fringes. The experience of the Lib–Lab pact left the Liberal Party with stronger confidence and experience to prepare for this, but the general election of 1979 removed the prospect at least for the time being.

Chapter 12

The Future

Britain has suffered a steady slide down the league table of successful industrial nations since the end of the Second World War. In the post-war Attlee parliament there was still a spirit of national reconstruction, but the thirty years 1950–80 have been sad ones for the country. Whatever statistic one cares to take to register prosperity, we have been slipping from being the richest or second richest country in Europe to being the second poorest. As an island nation of limited natural resources we have failed to adapt to the loss of empire in this period. We failed to adapt not only psychologically and politically, but also economically. We no longer have an automatic source of cheap raw materials and a ready market for our exports. For example in Kenya colony, where I was at school from 1949 to 1953, most of the trucks and motor cars were British with a few American and some French. Now in independent Kenya scarcely any are British. Most are German, French, Japanese and Italian.

In the twenty years 1953–73 manufacturing employment increased 11 per cent in France, 31 per cent in Germany, and a staggering 155 per cent in Japan. Over the same twenty years it fell by 13 per cent in the United Kingdom. We produce less while our imports rise. Our prices and delivery dates steadily push us out of world markets. This is a sure recipe for national bankruptcy, which has been staved off temporarily by the discovery of North Sea oil.

At the general election in 1979, using the experience of the Lib–Lab pact, the Liberal Party argued the case for a complete overhaul of our failed political system which had presided over this period. Liberals sought to secure a sufficient wedge in the new parliament to be able to bring this era to an end by holding the balance of power. Our argument did not fall on deaf ears and we survived the election in better shape than anyone forecast, but the siren appeal of the Tories for an outright majority proved stronger.

Yet our basic argument remained valid and indeed was taken up in an elegant and forceful manner by Roy Jenkins in his Dimbleby Lecture in November 1979. His analysis – like ours – concluded that our two-party system itself was ill-suited to our national requirements for the 1970s and 1980s.

The first damaging characteristic of our post-war politics has been that comparatively small changes in public opinion have led to violent switches in public policy of a kind not experienced by the multi-party democracies of Europe or the two-party democracy of the United States. The scale of the damage is difficult to quantify, but let me give some examples.

The British steel industry was nationalized by the Attlee government. It was denationalized by the Churchill government. It was renationalized by the Wilson government. Small bits were sold off to private enterprise by the Heath government and other bits may be sold by the Thatcher government. At the end of all this political horseplay we have a steel industry hopelessly uncompetitive which is having to be drastically cut down in size. The unions may be blamed and the management may be blamed but above all the politicians have ruined the industry. When it was in private hands no one would invest in it because of the threat of public takeover. When it was in public hands there was no long-term confidence or morale because of the threats of its dissolution. What a way to run and ruin an industry.

Or take prices and incomes policies. Tory and Labour governments have each come to power pledged against these, demolished whatever existed on coming into office and then repented and established new policies and machinery later. As a result no long-term policy on prices and incomes has gained acceptance in Britain. It has never really been tried. All we've had is a series of short-term measures of varying degrees of effectiveness which have been introduced by governments proclaiming they don't believe in them. The economic cost of lost opportunities in this field is incalculable.

Or take aid to industry. Most advanced democracies accept the need for some state investment agency to boost their economies. But in Britain we first set up the Industrial Reorganization Corporation and then abolished it. Then the National Enterprise Board was created and now looks like being largely destroyed. The Tories flex their muscles against such bodies while Labour seeks to use them to extend state control of the economy. There is no agreement on their proper and continuous function.

Amid the legions of waste created by alternating governments in expanding the public bureaucracy while the nation is less able to afford it, the setting up of the Land Commission in Newcastle one year and its abolition the next stands out as a particularly striking example.

Each government devotes much of its energy to undoing whatever its predecessor did, and nowadays the ink is not dry on a major parliamentary Bill before Her Majesty's Opposition is publicly pledged to repeal it. Each swing of the political pendulum threatens to take the country on yet more violently diverse directions to left and right. Thus the present 'non-interventionist' Tory government, more dogmatic and more doctrinaire than any previous Tory government, threatens to lead to a more left-wing socialist government than any previous Labour government. The political see-saw crashes up and down ever more violently to our discomfort.

It is not just that our minority two-party system dislocates the economy, but the parties are so composed that they are incapable of promoting national unity of purpose or industrial concord. They are still fighting the class war of the 1920s and 1930s. The Labour Party is financed by and controlled by the trade-union movement while the Tory Party is financed by and less obviously controlled by the interests of wealth and big business. Each looks after its own when in government and is opposed by the 'other side' of our society as being a wicked conspiracy interested only in its own kind.

These class-based attitudes pervade our housing, health and education policies as well as – and most directly – our industry. Against this background it is difficult to get a sane hearing for the long-standing Liberal policies of industrial partnership, still less for our new thinking on the need to link the concept of profit-sharing with incomes policy. Yet a policy of pulling together is surely worth trying in place of the policies of pulling apart which have manifestly failed.

The public money poured into British Leyland, for example, should have been conditional on a plant-by-plant productivity and profit-sharing scheme. The creation and just sharing of wealth is the only way to put Britain back on her feet. Yet what is economically necessary is politically impossible for our present party system to deliver.

There are two further dangers inherent in this failure. First, we look for scapegoats for our troubles. Hence persistent attacks on

the Common Market and our degree of official nastiness to immigrants. Second, any issues which fail to fall neatly into the two-party/
class battleground get ignored. Hence inadequate public policy on
conservation and energy developments, and on official secrecy and
public information. Economic and political failure has led to a growing sourness in our society, a turning inwards and a meanness to
others.

If we are to create a broader-based government capable once
again of harnessing public enthusiasm and creating a new national
mood of co-operation instead of bloody-mindedness we have to
change our rigid pattern of politics. Mrs Thatcher in opposition
was fond of denouncing Labour's phoney 'mandate for socialism'
based on the support of 29 per cent of the electorate in the October
1974 election. Now that she has come to power with the support
of 32 per cent that apparently transforms her 'mandate' into an
authentic one. Of course it doesn't. And no minority class-based
government of the kind we have had since 1945 can expect to
succeed.

I do not propose to rehearse here the litany of arguments for electoral reform. Its detractors claim that too much power would go
to minorities like the Liberals. Yet at present the two big parties
are private coalitions over whose actual policy directions the public
has little say. Electoral reform would enlarge their choices and
ensure an open coalition based on a public majority with authority
to run our affairs.

People in Britain are very accustomed to the alternation of the
Tory and Labour Parties in office. They know the system does not
work well but, such is the force of convention, they find it difficult
to imagine what could replace it.

We must have an electoral system which uses proportional representation to produce properly representative parliaments and
majority governments. By a chance, which I am glad we were able
to take advantage of, the Lib–Lab agreement provided a short but
successful spell of majority government.

We can no longer rely on flukes. That is why it is encouraging
that so many people inside and outside parliament, drawn from all
parties and none, now believe in electoral reform. The Campaign
for Electoral Reform makes an unanswerable case. I was particularly pleased that Roy Jenkins had lent his support to this vital
cause.

By the next general election I expect to see electoral reform as an issue which will attract wide cross-party support. This is not a narrow party matter for the Liberals and I have always welcomed new converts from whatever quarter they come.

Once we have electoral reform, we shall by definition have more broadly based majority government. This may take the form of a coalition between parties in which a common programme is agreed, even at the sacrifice of some ideological baggage. But it is often forgotten that under a PR system a party can conduct the government on its own if it meets one simple condition. It has to gain 50 per cent of the votes or more. Any party which gains 50 per cent will have to be a great deal wider and more popular in its appeal than anything we have seen in Britain for years. Either way we shall have governments which represent the majority and can genuinely speak for the people in the troubled years ahead.

I am often asked if I want realignment of the parties. The answer is that I do and that I believe a fair electoral system would help bring it about. The uneasy coalition inside the Labour Party particularly is only held together as a joint conspiracy to exploit the present electoral system in the pursuit of power.

As long as the interests of the rich and powerful demand political protection there will be a Conservative Party. The question is what the main opposition to it should be. It cannot continue to be an army of elderly place-seekers, financed by the trade unions, and dominated by a tiny unrepresentative group of Marxists.

During this parliament I intend to demonstrate that the only genuine alternative to the narrow policies of Tory dogma is the modern Liberal Party. I expect many Labour voters to join us as well as moderate Conservatives. I want to form a great alliance of progressives, radicals and social democrats with Liberal leadership, to change a rotten political system.

I am delighted that social democrats are beginning to realize that the present Labour Party is not their natural home. Our job in the Liberal Party is to persuade them to work together with us and to show them that we already exist as a movement of conscience and reform which they are looking for.

Our policies of decentralized government, strong local communities, environmental protection, co-operative industrial relations and a balanced sustainable economy, represent a real alternative as the country approaches the year 2000. We do not pretend we have all the answers but we have set the directions in which any progressive person should be searching.

As Tory policies fail, predictably but miserably, millions of people look for a better way. In local government, in by-elections and in opinion polls the Liberals gain strength. I want to see that we emerge as the alternative not just to the Thatcher government but to a discredited system of politics. We are angry and determined enough to lead the attack but I am enough of a realist to know that we cannot succeed without engaging the imagination and winning the support of thousands of political activists and millions of disillusioned voters. We have to show that there is a better way.

I do not see how any new 'centre party' could hope to beat the present system, though Liberals are always of course on the lookout for allies. The small 'l' liberal Tories are at present wholly in the grip of the mad ideologues of the right. The Labour Party's intellectual right has lost Roy Jenkins to Europe, Shirley Williams to defeat, John Mackintosh through death, David Marquand to the academic world, Dick Taverne to new party failure and Brian Walden to television. What is left is ill-equipped to oppose the strength of the hard left who at least have a credible if repugnant economic credo on offer.

The case for breaking out of the two-party straitjacket is overwhelming. In the eighteen months of the Lib–Lab pact the Liberals showed what could be achieved with even an unsatisfactory and belated fingerhold on power. If the electorate were to give the Liberals a firm grip I believe we could transform Britain's failure.

As a Liberal and a progressive in politics I want to see a lively diversity and influx of new ideas on our barren political scene. As a patriot, I want to see us agreeing where we can on the big issues that unite most sensible people and co-operating for the national advantage. I have believed for a long time that Britain is both a more diverse and, at root, a more united country than our political system allows us to express. That is why I have set as the next target for myself and my party the formation of a great government of reform after the next general election. Mrs Thatcher is fond of saying there is no choice between her reactionary brand of conservatism and the neo-marxism of the Labour left. The challenge to the Liberal Party is to show that she is wrong, as I am sure she is. There is another way.

From time to time there are watersheds in British politics when the nation stirs, shakes itself and sets off confidently in a new direction. These are our peaceful revolutions. Such a watershed year was 1906, as was 1945. I believe we are approaching another one and, indeed, that it is essential for our political and economic health that it comes soon.

The Liberal Party needs to take the lead, not just electorally but intellectually and morally, in convincing the majority of our fellow-citizens that there is a better and more balanced way forward – and one which offers hope.

We do not expect to achieve this without friends and allies. I want the debate to be about 'measures' and not just 'men'. A great government of reform cannot be built around the ambitions of a motley band of eminent politicians, however distinguished their past and however good their intentions. It needs a core of common purpose. It must represent a coming together of ideas and a shared dream of what might be.

It is in that spirit that I have put forward the outline of an agenda which could unite liberals, progressives and radicals with those social democrats and even conservatives who share our analysis. These policies are not based on ideology, whether it be monetarist or marxist. They are based, as is Liberalism itself, on common humanity. Britain still has one ace in its hand. The long years of Tory and Socialist paternalism have prevented us playing it. It is the inventiveness, the tolerance, the common sense – in fact the neglected genius – of the British people.

That is why my first criterion is that the policies of the government of national reform should be to bring the British together. The class-based parties have divided us for years when we should have been united. I cannot, for instance, think that everything the present government has done is wrong. But it is surely incontestable that, like its predecessors, it saw its first duty as looking after its own 'side'. This favouritism is built into the whole system of the upper-class party versus the working-class party, and the owner party versus the union party. There is a psychological pressure on people to take sides or be squeezed out of politics altogether.

The second criterion is whether the policies put forward go to the root of the matter, for that is the very definition of radicalism. We have had too many cosmetic coats of paint slapped on decaying institutions. The root causes of our decay have remained untouched through successive governments.

The final criterion is whether the policies are long-term rather than short-term. Since the war, we have had a surfeit of the sort of opportunism which is directed at the next election rather than the next decade. The changes in our world demand more strategic thinking and less hasty tacking from left to right and back again.

We need constitutional reform. Electoral reform is essential to a democratic representative system. Parliamentary reform is then required to allow the elected representatives to function properly. An effective and representative House of Commons would be the corner-stone of a reformed constitution which would also include a more broadly-based second chamber and a Bill of Rights.

Parties themselves should be characterized by democracy and openness. It is essential that the closed worlds of Westminster and Whitehall be opened to public scrutiny and understanding. Scandals of the sort that Bingham revealed over Rhodesian sanctions are the inevitable result of secrecy but the positive reasons for openness are strong as well.

The difficult challenges of the years ahead demand informed public participation. I believe that devolution of decision-making and decentralization of power are both part of rebuilding Britain on a more human and democratic basis.

Political problems often have economic symptoms which is why I put constitutional reform first. The main outlines of an alternative economic policy, however, can also be discerned.

Reform of industrial relations by introducing worker participation would enshrine the key role of the employee in the success and direction of our business, commerce and, most importantly, industry. Just as we should use democracy and participation to break down artificial barriers in politics, so we should also do the same in industry.

Monopoly union power too often misrepresents the employee's interests and entrenches historic divisions between capital and labour. Although many companies will never become co-operatives, the decision-making and profit-sharing of every enterprise should be based on co-operation. There can be agreement about incorporating profit-sharing into a more flexible incomes policy, which will help to defeat inflation and distribute wealth more fairly.

Reform of industrial relations and incomes policy should go hand in hand with an economic strategy which allows every company, business and individual to plan ahead. It should be based on the selective introduction of new technology, the conservation of energy and natural resources, and the development of a balanced and sustainable economy, including greater self-sufficiency in food. Reform cannot be realized by total state control for it needs the imagination and initiative of many new entrepreneurs. Equally, it will never come about with the sort of complacent policies we have at the moment, which are demolishing our industrial base daily while putting nothing in its place. We need the unconventional and experimental willingness to mix public and private enterprise which characterized Franklin Roosevelt's New Deal. Just as there are some secotrs boosting exports and earning foreign currency, such as high technology industry, where good productivity is essential, there are other labour-intensive small industries, such as home insulation programmes, which could provide high employment.

On the social front, too, it is no good the government demolishing the whole fabric of the welfare state in its zeal to cut public spending unless it is building other patterns of care to replace it. There could be a greatly increased role for the volunteer as well as more genuine community health schemes, but they depend in the first place on enlightened pump-priming.

Equally, the social security benefits jungle does not need random cutting back, but rather replacement by one integrated scheme of tax credits, so that each person, according to his or her circumstances, pays to, or recieves from the Exchequer one regular cheque.

I believe that such policies could unite most sensible people in the country and set us on the course towards a more satisfying and balanced way of life. The whole industrial world is looking for a new way forward and it would mean a great deal to people of my generation to think that Britain might become a part of the solution rather than a particularly intractable part of the problem. It would give us a valid international role, not just as a member of the politically united Europe which I hope for, but as part of the wider international community. The Brandt Commission's recommendations for a massive transfer of resources to the third world deserve support.

If sufficient men and women agree that these are our national priorities but that there is no hope of persuading the Labour and Conservative Parties to adopt them, the answer must lie in building a wider movement of reform which will. We should start creating it now.

That is why the Liberal hour has come again.

Appendix 1

1. *Mr Foot* welcomed members to the first meeting of the Government/Liberal Consultative Committee. He referred briefly to the procedural arrangements agreed with Mr Steel under which the bulk of the consultations between the Government and the Liberal party would be between individual Ministers and Liberal spokesmen. The initiative to consult could be taken by either party and the arrangement should operate as informally as possible. The outcome of such consultations need only be referred to the Committee if unresolved differences or problems arose. The Liberal party representatives welcomed this approach.

2. After a brief discussion the Committee agreed unanimously that:

   a. The Committee would meet once a fortnight. Wednesdays at 7.15pm would be particularly convenient for the Liberals because it followed on from their own Parliamentary Party meeting. It would also tie in with the release of information about business in the House for the week ahead.

   b. The agenda for meetings would be agreed between the head of Mr Steel's office and the Private Secretary to the Lord President.

   c. The scope of any statement to the Press would be agreed at the end of each meeting. The most which would be released was confirmation that a meeting had taken place and the subject headings of the items discussed. The content of discussions and any conclusions reached would remain confidential and would not be released.

3. *Mr Foot* said that it would be helpful if the consultations between the Liberal spokesman and the Secretary of State for Industry about industrial democracy in the Post Office could take place as soon as possible. *Mr Pardoe* said that their spokesman was meeting Post Office Union representatives that evening and would then be able to arrange an early meeting with the Secretary of State.

4. There was a brief discussion on the following matters, which were raised by the Liberal representatives:

   a. the provision of a list of the Bills and Orders in the pipeline. *Mr Foot* said he would see if this could be provided but information about all Orders might not be readily available.

   b. Arrangements for the Direct Elections Bill. *Mr Rees* said that the Bill would be published on Friday with a debate some time after Easter. He undertook to arrange a discussion with Mr Jeremy Thorpe as soon as possible.

c. The timing of the Housing Finance Review. *Mr Foot* said that he would advise when information about this review was likely to be available; he thought it would not be for some weeks yet.

5. *Mr Pardoe* referred to the current Tory game of asking whether the Liberals were in Opposition or in Government. He wondered whether the new consultative arrangements would cause the Tories to raise difficulties about the composition of House Committees. Mr Cocks advised that the key factor in terms of party strengths in committees was the issue of the Whip. The Tories had argued in the case of Mr Stonehouse, Mr Sillars and Mr Robertson, that as they had ceased to receive the Labour Whip they could not be included in the Labour strength. They could not reverse that argument now.

6. *Mr Hooson* asked what were the vital issues for the Government at the present time. It was essential that misunderstandings did not arise about the importance that the Government attached to a particular matter. He referred to the Liberal vote against the Government in the defence debate and said that in the event their action had not led to a Government defeat. *Mr Cocks* said that it would be difficult to formalise a list of matters requiring particular care. Supply days could be difficult but in general the legislation in the pipeline from the Lords was uncontentious. He thought that the right approach would be to maintain good communications between the Whips.

7. *Mr Pardoe* said that the Liberal party would vote against budget resolutions numbers 11 and 15 which concerned increases in petrol and vehicle and excise duty. The total sum to be raised by the increases proposed was £360m. The Liberals had been on record in previous budget debates for their strong opposition to increased petrol prices and over licences because of the effect on rural areas, traditionally low earning areas, where it was often particularly important to own a car to get to work. *Mr Pardoe* said he would be discussing the matter with the Chief Secretary (Mr Barnett) on Thursday 31 March at 2.45pm. The Liberals would support other means of raising a similar sum of money. *Mr Foot* said that he would discuss the Liberals' intentions with colleagues.

Appendix 2

Note of a Meeting between The Lord President and Mr David Steel, Room 4, 26 September 1977 at 4.00pm

Mr Steel met the Lord President to run generally over the legislative ground for the coming Session so that he would be aware as early as possible before the next meeting of the Consultative Committee on 19 October of possible developments in policy areas in which the Liberal Party might wish to contribute. It would also assist him in preparing for the Liberal Party Conference to be aware of the constraints on the legislative timetable. The *Lord President* emphasised that much of what he would say was on a confidential and informal basis since discussions on the legislative timetable were still in progress.

The *Lord President* outlined the timetable:

a) Three constitutional Bills (Scotland, Wales and Direct Elections) which in all would take *36 days*, allowing slightly less time than in the 1976–77 Session for devolution (and indicating an early guillotine motion).

b) Essential Bills, *14 days* (Broadcasting, Transport, Civil Aviation, Power Stations, Atomic Energy, Continental Shelf, Participation Agreements, Trustee Savings Banks, Weights and Measures, Solomon Islands Independence, Company Law).

c) Top priority Bills (Shipbuilding Industry, Inner Cities, Housing help for First Time Buyers) taking *5 days*.

This meant 55 days for Government Bills in additon to the 15 days allowed for the Finance etc Bills. *If* an autumn Finance Bill were to be introduced, this would mean finding 6 days from the above business.

The Lord President went on to describe the Bills the Government would like to mention in the Queen's Speech and get through the House if time allowed. He would welcome Liberal views on these, especially any they particularly would prefer, at the Consultative Committee. These Bills are:

a) *Merchant Shipping*, which has the support of the interest groups concerned, is a long standing commitment and should not prove too controversial;

b) *Post Office Workers*, on which preliminary discussions have been held with the Liberals but the Government would welcome Mr Hooson's discussing this with the Attorney General, who had some points to put;

c) *Employment and Training*, decentralisation of the MSC;

d) *Medical*, to implement recommendations of the Merrison and Briggs Reports;

e) *Education Bill*

f) *Suppression of Terrorism*, to give support to international agreements;

g) *Crown Agents*, which might need to be made Essential category;

h) *Local Government Functions*, which would partially restore to e.g. Bristol and Plymouth, functions taken over by the County Councils under the 1972 legislation. No Government decision has been taken as yet on the policy merits of this;

i) *Northern Ireland Judicature*, to reform and restructure the Courts Service;

j) *Consumer Protection*, still under discussion;

k) *Official Secrets*, which raises a number of difficult issues, not least what any Bill should contain that would not be more restrictive than present legislation. *Mr Steel* said that he himself would be content with a White Paper being produced, as earnest of the Government's good intentions, but felt that the majority of his colleagues would wish to press for a Bill this Session;

l) *Film Industry*, which the Government would like to mention;

m) *Multiple Registration*, which needs further discussion with the Liberals;

n) *Domestic Proceedings in Magistrates' Courts*, which in Mr Steel's view should extend also to Scotland since much hardship is caused there because of the prevention of actions in the Sheriff Courts;

o) *Registration of Business Names*

p) *House of Commons Administration*, which need not be this Session;

q) *Public Lending Right*, which could probably be turned into a non-statutory scheme;

r) *Hare Coursing*, which might go to a Private Member;

s) *Electricity Supply*

t) *Local Government Attendance Allowances*, on which the Robinson Report is still wanted.

In initial reaction, *Mr Steel* said nothing alarmed him in this list but he would need to consult his colleagues. He mentioned seat belts, which could be put into a miscellaneous provisions Transport Bill.

However, *Mr Steel* emphasised the importance to the Liberals of inclusion of the profit-sharing element in the Finance Bill. The Prime Minister had expressed concern that this would overload the Finance Bill, and Mr Joel Barnett had confirmed that the six or so clauses would take some extra Parliamentary time. *Mr Steel* said he would give these clauses priority over other possible legislation in the coming Session because:-

    a) the Liberals had agreed a form of wording with the Chief Secretary and,

    b) reaction to the Lib–Lab Pact within the Liberal Party has made it clear to him that the Liberals need to show one specific proposal in legislation as having originated from the Liberals.

Consequently, *Mr Steel* acknowledged that they might have to sacrifice other desirable measures in the legislative programme, but on this he would need to consult his colleagues.

In conclusion *Mr Steel* mentioned the dissatisfaction amongst his colleagues that the Liberals had not been sufficiently fore-warned of the announcement appointing Mr Lever to make a special study of the problems affecting small businesses. Despite an internal hold-up in the Liberals' offices, *Mr Steel* agreed with his colleagues that this had been an unfortunate incident; if the Liberals were to claim any credit in an area of special concern they would need to be in a position to issue an almost simultaneous press notice. He asked particularly to be kept well informed of any developments on the profit-sharing arrangements so that the Liberals could claim suitable credit.

Appendix 3

Letter from the Secretary of the Lib–Lab Consultative Committee

Privy Council Office
Whitehall, London SW1A 2AT
30 September 1977

Rt Hon. David Steel MP
House of Commons
London SW1

You asked for a note of the Bills discussed at your meeting with the Lord President on Monday. You readily agreed that this would be sent on a personal basis and that the total list is for your eyes only. As the Lord President explained, the proposed programme is still under active consideration and changes may be made in the scope of some Bills.

Arrangements have been made for the Consultative Committee to meet in Room 4 in the House at 2.00pm on 19 October, when the main item on the agenda will be the Liberal views on the proposed Bills, particularly those which we have shown in Category three. But the Lord President hopes that you will continue to raise any matters of interest to you or your colleagues as they occur.

Category One
Three constitutional Bills:

    a) Scotland
    b) Wales
    c) Direct Elections to the European Assembly

Category Two
Essential Bills which must be fitted in next Session for financial, legal, international or other reasons:

    a) *Broadcasting Bill*, required to renew the IBA Act 1973 before its expiry.

    b) *Transport Bill*, required for financial reasons, to increase limits on passenger service grants to BR and to provide for the financial reconstruction of the NFC; will also be used to implement the proposals in the recent White Paper on public transport plans, bus licensing, heavy lorries, and possibly the control of private car parks and parking space.

    c) *Civil Aviation Bill*, required to increase the borrowing power of the CAA. Other provisions could include: airport security charges, the post-Laker situation, and the enforcement of tariffs. On these latter two, I understand that Mr Pardoe has advised that the Liberals would not feel able to support them and the Lord President will be interested to know whether this means that they would abstain or vote against.

d) *Power Stations (Financial Arrangements) Bill*, required to provide the necessary legislative authority to pay compensation to the CEGB for advancing Drax B.

e) *Atomic Energy Bill*, to confer powers of entry on inspectors of the International Atomic Energy Agency, required to implement UK obligations under the UK/Euratom/IAEA Agreement for the application of safeguards in the UK in connection with the Non-Proliferation Treaty, enabling this Agreement to be brought into force.

f) *Continental Shelf Bill*, required for reasons of financial propriety, to provide express statutory cover for the Department of Energy contribution to the MOD costs of patrolling oil and gas fields.

g) *Participation Agreements Bill*, urgently required to exempt oil participation agreements from the Restrictive Trade Practices Act, under which certain provisions of such agreements might otherwise be declared void.

h) *Weights and Measures Bill*, required next Session or – at latest – the Session after; to provide for the changeover from the minimum to the average contents system for pre-packed goods, as required by EEC directives.

i) *Trustees Savings Banks Bill*, required to give TSBs powers to grant mortgages which it was thought they had (some mortgages have already been granted).

j) *Company Law Bill*. Essential next Session to implement the EEC second Directive on this subject. The proposed registration of Business Names Bill – which provides for the raising of fees to make the Register self-supporting – will probably be tacked on. The addition of other company law provisions is being considered e.g. on insider dealing.

k) *Solomon Islands Independence Bill*

It is expected that these Bills would take up 14 days.

Category Three

Other Bills, which Departmental Ministers wish included in the legislative programme and which might be mentioned in the Queen's Speech.

a) *Shipbuilding Industry*. The Government is committed to giving financial support for a shipbuilding redundancy scheme. A short Bill is needed to provide for the necessary payments, with effect from 1 July 1977.

b) *Inner Cities*. This would implement the promise of legislation given in the inner cities White Paper to enhance the powers of certain local authorities to assist industry.

c) *Housing*. Legislation to help first time home buyers. Another provision – still under discussion – is to increase the Housing Corporation Guarantee powers to raise private capital.

NOTE: These three Bills are top priority to be mentioned in the Queen's Speech and will take up five days.

d) *Merchant Shipping*. Badly needed reform of law relating primarily to safety and conditions of work at sea. Wanted by both unions and industry and the Government is firmly committed to legislating as soon as practicable.

e) *Post Office Workers*. To ensure that they have the right to take normal industrial action. The Lord President mentioned to you that he would welcome Mr Hooson's discussing this further with the Attorney General.

f) *Employment and Training*. Decentralisation of MSC; power to take new measures against unemployment without the need for primary legislation; and (if agreement can be reached among those concerned) arrangements for collective funding of industrial training.

g) *Medical*. To implement the Merrison Committee recommendations on the reconstitution of GMC. Also some of the recommendations in the Briggs Report e.g. the reorganisation of the machinery for the Nurses, Health Visitors and Midwives Professions.

h) *Education*. Would include provisions on parental choice, industrial scholarships and grants, and the Taylor Committee recommendations on school governors (but the scope of the Bill is still under discussion).

i) *Suppression of Terrorism*. To give effect to the European Convention on this subject. Of international importance. We have been publicly urging other countries to ratify.

j) *Crown Agents*. To confer corporate status on the Crown Agents. The forthcoming Fay Report may stimulate pressure for action and this Bill may need to go into Essential category.

k) *Local Government Functions*. Policy is still under consideration but the Bill would partially restore to certain firm county boroughs (e.g. Bristol, Plymouth) functions taken from them under the 1972 legislation.

l) *Northern Ireland Judicature*. Major reorganisation of higher courts, on lines of Beeching reforms in England and Wales.

m) *Protection of the Consumer*. Scope still under discussion but could include consumer safety; fair trading; and perhaps banking and deposit taking institutions, also credit unions.

n) *Official Secrets Acts.* The Lord President explained the difficulties which had been encountered in drawing up detailed proposals and that the next step might be a White Paper.

o) *Film Industry.* To raise the limit on public funds for the NFFC.

p) *Multiple Registration.* To implement 1973 Speaker's Conference recommendation preventing second home owners from registering at more than one place. The Lord President mentioned that this would require further discussions with your colleagues.

q) *Domestic Proceedings in Magistrates' Courts.* To carry over into domestic proceedings in magistrates' courts the changes made when the divorce laws were reformed.

r) *House of Commons (Administration).* Implementation of the Bottomley Committee Report – need not be this Session but could be fitted in if a convenient slot emerged.

s) *Public Lending Right* – but the possibility of a non statutory scheme is under consideration.

t) *Hare Coursing* – which might go to a Private Member.

u) *Electricity Supply Industry* – which would reorganise the industry, the aim being to enable it to provide better direction and corporate planning.

v) *Local Government (Attendance) Allowances.* Changes in the system of allowances for councillors.

CAROLYN MORRISON (Miss)
Privy Council Office

Appendix 4

Liberal Shadow Administration

*Lord Avebury	Energy, and Race Relations
Lord Banks CBE	Social Services
Alan Beith MP	Chief Whip, and Education
*The Rt Hon. Lord Byers CBE	Leader in the Lords
Clement Freud MP	Northern Ireland, and Broadcasting and the Arts
The Rt Hon. Jo Grimond MP	No Portfolio
Emlyn Hooson QC, MP	Defence and the Law
Geraint Howells MP	Wales, and Agriculture
Russell Johnston MP	Scotland (and Member in European Parliament)
*Lord Mackie CBE	No Portfolio
John Pardoe MP	Treasury
David Penhaligon MP	Transport and Environmental Matters (Employment and Energy Matters in Commons)
Stephen Ross MP	Housing and Local Government
Baroness Seear	Employment, and Prices and Consumer Protection
The Rt Hon. David Steel MP	Leader
The Rt Hon. Jeremy Thorpe MP	Foreign and Commonwealth
Richard Wainwright MP	Trade and Industry
Lord Wigoder QC	Chief Whip in the Lords
*Lord Winstanley	Health

(* denotes former Member of the Commons)

Appendix 5

Extract from Note of a Meeting with Baroness Seear Held at the Department of Employment on Friday 7 October 1977

Present: Secretary of State for Employment
Mr Wake
Mrs Kent
Baroness Seear

1. *Baroness Seear* confirmed that she would act as principal employment spokesman for the Liberals. Mr Penhaligon would speak on employment matters in the Commons.

2. *Baroness Seear* said that the Liberals attached enormous importance to Government policy on pay, particularly the 10 per cent guidelines. They were very concerned about a possible breach of the guidelines by Ford's. Naturally, many employers would prefer to give way and could pay; many firms e.g. ICI felt that they were losing skilled workers because they could not pay enough. However, it was essential that they should hold the line. Ford's workers were not low paid and there was no justification for their breaching the policy. It was essential to the continuance of the pact with the Liberals that the Government should stand firm on the Ford negotiations.

3. *The Secretary of State* said that he had limited sympathy with the argument that employers were losing workers because of poor pay: there were always other reasons. But even without that argument, Ford's was a very difficult case. The repercussions of a high settlement could spread right across industry, not just within car firms. He had talked to Moss Evans of the TGWU about pay policy and the TGWU's attitude, but the Union held that they were adhering to the TUC line – i.e. support for the 12 month rule but no more. The TGWU considered that in the post-phase II period there was no agreement with the Government so that they were entitled to pursue free collective bargaining to get the most they could without jeopardising jobs of their members. The TGWU were not party to the pact with the Liberals and did not recognise it as a constraint.

Appendix 6

Note of the Sixth Meeting of the Government/Liberal Consultative Committee – Room 4, House of Commons, at 3pm Tuesday 18 October 1977

Present:

Rt Hon. Michael Foot MP

Rt Hon. Michael Cocks MP

Sir Freddie Warren

Mr J W Stevens

Mr Alan Beith MP

Mr Emlyn Hooson MP

Mr John Pardoe MP

THE FORTHCOMING LEGISLATIVE PROGRAMME

Mr Foot stressed that the major Constitutional Bills to which the Government was committed – Direct Elections, the Scotland and Wales Bills – and other Bills (some of which he mentioned), essential for financial, legal or international reasons, left very little time for any other Bills. The Government gave top priority, in the remaining time, to three Bills, the *Shipbuilding Industry*, *Inner Cities* and *Housing* (to provide assistance to first time house buyers). There were a number of measures which the Government favoured, but which did not appear in the programme for lack of time. Any references to them would be made obliquely, possibly in the speeches of the Prime Minister and other Government spokesmen. *Mr Foot* went on to remark that such a consultation as this on the content of the Queen's Speech was abnormal, and especially so before Cabinet had taken final decisions, so he counted on the confidentiality of the discussions. He would welcome, however, Liberal views and any representations on individual measures would be taken into account.

Mr Pardoe said he and his colleagues fully appreciated the unusual nature of this consultative meeting, and would say generally and publicly that the Liberals were pressing the Government on various measures. The Liberals' initial reaction to the package was that all the Bills, including the clutch of 'possibles', added up to an unexciting programme, especially for English voters, and looked electorally dull for the Labour Party. He suggested that the Government (who appreciated Liberal concern on this point) should find something to stir English hearts and include it in the programme.

Sir Freddie Warren emphasised that the Session was already overcrowded, and any autumn finance package would add to the difficulties of timing.

Mr Hooson then went on to say that the Liberal Party felt strongly that some things ought to be mentioned in the Queen's Speech, and felt equally strongly that others should not. They wanted an *identifiably Liberal measure*, and chose a *Land Act* to establish a Land Bank. *Mr Howells* had discussed this with Mr John Silkin, who he said was agreed in principle. It would not be a large Bill, it would not require much Parliamentary time, and support could be given through existing Banks. For the Liberals, second to the Conservative Party in some 70 seats in the last election, and with 50 of these in rural areas, such a measure might swing the electoral scales, and not be damaging to Labour.

Mr Hooson went on to say that Liberal activists were very concerned about an *Official Secrets Bill*. The Parliamentary Party accepted that this was a most complicated issue, and had agreed that the issue of a White Paper would first be necessary, and now they would press for this to be put into the Queen's Speech, with the additional undertaking that the White Paper would presage a debate and legislation, though with no commitment to legislating this Session. On the *Post Office Bill*, on which he had had discussions with the Attorney General, the Liberals would find it very difficult to support the Government, and would argue in any case for criminality to be removed. They found this area contentious, and in particular found it difficult to define a trade dispute separately from a political dispute.

Mr Foot, in reply, said the Government would look immediately at the possibilities of a Land Act, and inform the Liberals. The line proposed on Official Secrets accorded with the Government's thinking, but the Government were strongly committed to changing the Post Office Acts. Clearly they would need to discuss this further with the Liberals in an effort to persuade them of the correctness of the policy.

Mr Beith said that the Liberals supported strongly a number of other possible Bills:

(a) *Consumer Protection;*
(b) *First Time House Buyers;*
(c) *Education* – implementing the Taylor Report and parental choice;
(d) *Multiple Registration* which, if it disappeared from the programme, they would regard as a breach of faith. Furthermore, coming as it would near the end of the Government's term of office, it should be promoted to prevent the Conservatives capturing more marginal seats.

Mr Foot said it was not clear at this stage how quickly a Bill on *Consumer Protection* could be got ready – it might be that a Bill ready soon would be weaker than was desirable, or otherwise too large for a crowded Session. *First Time House Buyers* was already included. The *Education Bill* was not included to date in the legislative programme because there would be no time. The Government were not so confident that it would be non-controversial, and a possibility for Second Reading Committee, and even if it started in the Lords this would not relieve the pressure on Commons' time. *Multiple Registration* needed further consideration since the Government were not so clear that all the obstacles had been removed. For instance where student votes were concerned.

Mr Beith said there were other measures which the Liberals would like to see mentioned:

(a) Profit-sharing
(b) Reduction of the direct tax burden
(c) Small Businesses and the self-employed,

on which there was substantial agreement with the Government. If mentioned in the Queen's Speech both the Government and the Liberals could claim the credit.

(d) Youth and unemployment
(e) Co-operative Development Agency.

Mr Foot said discussions were in progress on how Profit-sharing could be announced; it would not be appropriate to mention (b) in the Queen's Speech, but rather in another, probably economic, debate; (c) would be mentioned though not necessarily with a promise of legislation. On (d) and (e) the Government would check on progress.

Mr Beith said there were serious areas of difficulty for the Liberals. Already mentioned was the *Post Office*; the *Civil Aviation Bill* was another – *Mr Foot* said the two points of difficulty had been removed – and the *Power Stations* (*Financial Arrangements*), where the Liberals were puzzled by the CEGB last weekend saying they wanted more capacity by 1980, but yet were unwilling to pay for DRAX, and were forcing the Government to pay. *Occupational Pensions Schemes** would also be opposed.

Mr Foot said the DRAX B Bill must go through and he hoped that Lord Avebury would clear up the Liberal worry, to their satisfaction, at his meeting the next morning with Mr Benn. The Occupational Pensions Scheme had been discarded.

Mr Beith said of the various other Bills discussed with Liberal spokesmen they were not opposed, but did not see them as essential. For instance, they did not accord high priority to *Merchant Shipping*, *Trustee Savings Banks* and *Broadcasting*.

Mr Foot explained that the Merchant Shipping Bill was a long-standing commitment which would be attractive to those in the industry, and

---

* The Occupational Pension Scheme Bill had been discussed frequently between Lord Banks and Stan Orme. We opposed it successfully because it simply sought to provide for trade union nominees on the boards of pension funds, and was a further extension of Labour's gift of patronage to the trade union leaders.

although most of the 'possible measures' appealed to minority groups, this was an important one. Mr Foot was unaware of any developments which suggested the TSB legislation would not be needed and promised to check. The *Company Law Bill* would implement EEC directives, but he noted that the Liberals were opposed to tacking on too many other proposals, such as Insider Trading.

Mr Pardoe returned to the *Post Office Bill* – he said it would be seen, in the context of the Grunwick dispute, as an enabling issue. More serious would be the coming battle over the Police and the right to strike, on which the public were likely to be more sympathetic. *Mr Foot* understood this concern but still hoped he could get agreement with the Liberals since he saw the Government as committed on the postal workers. He was glad to have had this exchange of views and would further consider how this might be dealt with in the Queen's Speech.

OTHER ITEMS

Mr Beith mentioned the scheme he had proposed for *probationary teachers* and said he was most unhappy at the bureaucratic reasons given for not implementing it, and would be pursuing this further with Mrs Williams.

Mr Hooson and *Mr Pardoe* asked if there had been any developments on the *construction industry*, where help might be given for example by sponsoring Council house repair under the RSG now, and not waiting for next April, and promoting private house insulation. This was a high Liberal priority, as was also ensuring fair distribution of the RSG so that *rural areas* were not discriminated against. *Mr Foot* said the Government were watching these areas carefully and needed to relate them to help for Inner City areas. He also noted the Liberal view that there would be great political advantage in having a *Christmas bonus for pensioners.*

Sir Freddie Warren said he would be writing to Mr Beith on the plans for next Wednesday's sitting of the House.

Date of Next Meeting: This was provisionally agreed for 11am Wednesday 26 October in the same room.

C R MORRISON (Miss)
Privy Council Office
19 October 1977

Appendix 7

Extract from a Meeting on Wednesday 26 October

INDIVIDUAL ITEMS FROM THE PREVIOUS MEETING

1. LAND BANK

Mr Foot said that he had made soundings immediately after the last meeting because he thought that to include the Land Bank in the Queen's Speech at this stage would be a very long shot. He had now concluded it would not be possible, though this was not to denigrate the policy. Much more thought and consultation would be needed. *Mr Hooson* said that he understood that Joel Barnett, talking to Geraint Howells, had mentioned that there would be something in the Queen's Speech on agricultural credit. *Mr Foot* thought this would not be so, and in addition he thought that Mr Howells was not pressing for commitment to a Land Bank Bill in the Queen's Speech. *Mr Beith* also said he thought the idea needed further development. *Mr Pardoe* suggested that what Mr Hooson had mentioned was probably relating to investment in agriculture in the Chancellor's statement.

In any case *Mr Hooson* stressed the importance of the Land Bank proposals as a high Liberal priority, needing the commitment of the Government in the Queen's Speech. *Mr Foot* reiterated this would not appear but this in no way meant that the Government would not continue to discuss it with a view to future action. *Mr Hooson* said that the Liberals needed to sell the Queen's Speech as having demonstrable Liberal measures, since there were large numbers of supporters ready to denounce the Pact. Even if the Agricultural Credit Corporation could be modified, a sensible move, this need not rule out grants *and* credit facilities. *Mr Foot* undertook to send a letter describing the situation, and *Mr Cocks* stressed that the Queen's Speech was a 'starter' and that subsequent speeches, both from the Government front benches and from the Liberals, could work in Liberal measures and influence.

2. EDUCATION BILL

Mr Foot said it was possible that the Prime Minister would refer to this Bill in his speech as a desirable measure he would like to see enacted were there time, for the same reasons as the Liberals would like. There were other measures similarly placed, which would not appear in the Queen's Speech. *Mr Beith* regretted this – the *minimum* desirable would be a reference in the Prime Minister's speech. *Mr Foot* said he regretted this but again it was pressure of time, which could not be overcome. *Mr*

Cocks remarked that the Taylor Report had not long been out and the Prime Minister's reference would show progress while *Mrs Williams* was considering it further.

3. MULTIPLE REGISTRATION

Mr Foot said he was puzzled, as were the Home Office, by the Liberals' feeling that not to introduce a Bill this session would be a 'breach of faith'. The Bill was not in the programme since there were still some details to be examined further, but this again did not mean that the Government did not think it a good measure. *Mr Beith* said he thought that all were at the second stage of agreeing its content; that Home Office Ministers had agreed to legislation, and that because it would be a small Bill it could find a place as a measure of political interest, especially to the Government.

Mr Foot said he would take these points into account. He could not promise to have it included in the Queen's Speech, but he undertook to look afresh at it to see if it could go forward. If there were any difficulties he would come back and discuss these and in the meantime look again at the previous discussions. *Mr Beith* was grateful but again wondered at why the Government seemed prepared to leave a political/electoral advantage with the Conservative Party.

Mr Hooson left at this point.

4. CONSUMER PROTECTION

Mr Foot said there would be a reference in the Queen's Speech to an improvement in competition policy but there would be no Bill of any substance in the Session. *Mr Pardoe* asked what sort of Bill, and *Mr Foot* said probably a minor one, not extending as far as the Liberals would hope, and even with this Bill there would be no definite commitment this Session. *Mr Pardoe* understood the timetable problem; competition policy was dear to Liberal hearts, as it was also to DPCP [Department of Press and Consumer Protection], and therefore the phrases in the Queen's Speech would be helpful, but how could the Liberals take credit for *no* legislation?

5. PROFIT-SHARING

Mr Beith stressed that it was paramount for the Liberals that profit-sharing be mentioned in the Queen's Speech, and David Steel had mentioned this to the Prime Minister. He said that they viewed this as a commitment agreed with the Government and not competing with the Land Bank as a high priority. Would the Queen's Speech mention the forthcoming White Paper? *Mr Foot* would give no commitment on this as it was still under discussion.

6. TRUSTEE SAVINGS BANKS

Mr Beith said they were fully in favour of this and were happy to have affirmed that the Treasury thought it desirable and essential.

7. EMPLOYMENT APPEAL

Mr Foot outlined the difficulties which had been encountered, particularly with the Conservatives, in drafting the appeal. Because of this it would probably take place early in 1978. *Mr Beith* said the Liberals were putting pressures on Lady Seear and David Steel to push the Conservatives along, and would do so more vigorously, but *Mr Foot* suggested they wait until he finds out the latest position from Mr Booth, who would be having talks early in the Session with the other Parties, including the Nationalists.

8. POST OFFICE BILL

Mr Foot recalled the hostile reception this Bill had been given by the Liberals at the previous Consultative Committee. He said it *was* mentioned in the Queen's Speech, since the Government viewed it as important, but that there would probably be no time for legislation. He would like the Liberals to discuss this urgently to see if they could be persuaded of the merits of the Bill. The Government were fully committed to the principle of this Bill.

9. COMPANIES BILL

Mr Foot said this would be referred to in the Queen's Speech. He noted the Liberal dislike of tacking on too many extra provisions.

10. MERCHANT SHIPPING

Mr Beith asked if the Merchant Shipping Bill would be mentioned, and *Mr Foot* said this was likely, since the Bill has many merits, including pay policy ones, but whether or not there would be legislative time was uncertain. *Mr Beith* said they supported this Bill *except for* the section on foreign takeovers. *Mr Foot* said the Bill would not be an immediate starter so there would be ample time for discussion of this point.

11. OCCUPATIONAL PENSIONS

One again *Mr Foot* said the Liberals were misguided in their opposition to this Bill but that the Government would not be proceeding this Session with it.

ADDITIONAL ITEM – NATIONAL EFFICIENCY AUDIT

Mr Pardoe mentioned briefly the apparent all-Party agreement that present methods of expenditure control were open to review. Some form of National Efficiency Audit seemed a viable proposition, as a means of continually monitoring public expenditure, and *Mr Pardoe* asked if proposals (by, for example, Mr Du Cann) to amalgamate the PAC and Expenditure Committees might assist in such a reform.

Mr Foot, in reply, said this was a very large subject, which would take time to consider. He asked if the Liberals had put forward views to the Procedure Committee, since it was also very much a matter for the House. The area of control of public expenditure was crucial, but all proposals for change would need very careful consideration from many angles before any specific reform could be decided on. All Liberal contributions would of course be welcomed and discussed. *Mr Pardoe* agreed to consider this subject further.

Appendix 8

Note of the Ninth Meeting of the Government/Liberal Consultative Committee – Room 4, House of Commons, at 8.30pm Wednesday, 18 January and 7.30pm Thursday, 19 January 1978

Present:

Rt Hon. Michael Foot MP

Rt Hon. Michael Cocks MP

Rt Hon. Merlyn Rees MP

Rt Hon. Joel Barnett MP

Rt Hon. John Silkin MP

Mr Alan Beith MP

Mr Emlyn Hooson MP

Mr John Pardoe MP

Mr Geraint Howells MP

Sir Freddie Warren

Mr J W Stevens

THE GREEN POUND

The meeting had been called to discuss the views of the Liberals on proposals to devalue the Green Pound, and especially how their Early Day Motion 91 related to Government thinking.

Mr Pardoe began by explaining that the figure of 10% in the Motion was carefully inserted in order to ensure a vote with such a figure in mind, as was the Conservatives' $7\frac{1}{2}$%.

Mr Silkin agreed that 10% looked about right for the beef and pigmeat industries, but asked if 10% was a flexible figure, not one to be implemented immediately or with a specific time-scale in mind. We must bear in mind also that other sectors of the farming industry were not so badly affected.

Mr Hooson said that 10% must be seen as a Liberal commitment over the 12-month period but agreed it need not come all at once. Would it be possible to be selective and benefit pigs and beef?

Mr Silkin explained it would not be acceptable to other EEC Ministers for the UK to 'pick and choose'.

Mr Barnett expanded further; it would be difficult to commit the UK in advance of the negotiations with too precise a figure and its timing, especially as much would depend on price-fixing and beef returns.

Mr Hooson warned that if the Government would give no commitment on Monday they faced a real possibility of being defeated.

Mr Howells pointed out that the Liberal Early Day Motion had been tabled last December, and that it was a Conservative choice of Agriculture for the Supply Day on Monday. A motion of no confidence would be likely, and even a demand for an immediate devaluation, if no figures were produced by the Government.

Mr Barnett agreed the Government must find a formula which also left the Minister as free a hand in Brussels as possible.

Mr Silkin said that although the precise terms of Monday's motion are not known it would presumably include $7\frac{1}{2}\%$ now, and the Government would need to table an amendment offering some money now and more later. To some extent the Government's hands would be tied – the proposal would need to be an EEC one, put to them next Monday or Tuesday, but we should need to know before the weekend if some such proposal would be put. Otherwise we would get into the price-fixing period and the next possible date would be the beginning of the Marketing Year around 1 May.

Mr Rees asked whether the Liberals would accept a formula of some money now and a general commitment of more later? The *Liberals* said no, they would seek a precise figure, but they would accept an approach within that of some now, more later.

Mr Silkin pointed out that devaluation was a blunt instrument, benefiting some sectors not needing it, and that also we needed to take price-fixing into account. He would like to keep the common price as low as possible but a realistic assumption might be anything up to 5%. It was difficult at this stage to fix on a figure for devaluation without knowing this pricing figure. Hence the Liberals' 10% was about right in quantity but not necessarily from devaluation.

Mr Hooson said that we would need to find a formula for arriving at 10% over the year but argued that money was needed on the table now. He did not agree with the view that the amendment by the Government might concede the principle of relief, especially for beef and pigs, but not mention a figure.

Mr Silkin saw the force of the Liberals' 10% over the year, in the context of pay guidelines, but returned to the difficulties of phasing this in relation both to price-fixing and devaluation. The Government had as yet no amendment worked out for next Monday's debate but welcomed this chance to appreciate Liberal views.

Mr Pardoe outlined the various options:

a) the figure has to be 10%

b) 'this year' would be interpreted in several ways,

c) as could how the 10% might be phased, but

d) the Liberals demanded money on the table now, a commitment of 10% for the whole year, with phasing as was practical from the Government's point of view.

In short, the Government would need to return with a formula which included a minimum on the table now.

Mr Silkin stressed again that price-fixing needed to be taken into account in the calculation of the 10%, and that too precise a commitment would make negotiation difficult in the course of the year.

The meeting was adjourned until 7.30 the following night.

Mr Barnett and Mr Hooson were absent on 19 January.

Mr Silkin resumed by saying he appreciated the Liberal demands and saw that 5% now would be a reasonable figure. He would have to ask the Commission for an immediate devaluation if we reached agreement at this meeting, and this would need to be done on Friday 20th for consideration in Brussels the following Tuesday. Any subsequent amendment in Monday's debate would need to leave his hands as free as possible for negotiation over the next twelve months, and he produced a form of words for discussion.

Mr Pardoe pointed out that if sterling did not continue to improve then a further devaluation would almost certainly be required. What would the Government do in May if income improvement for the pig industry had only risen 7%? *Mr Silkin* said 3% would be lacking *on average* and some of this would come in sterling improvement.

Mr Howells discussed the proposed amendment; he wanted 'by an appreciable figure' altered to read more specifically 'by at least 10%' and accepted that a devaluation of 5% now and a price-fixing adjustment of 2% would be a reasonable step forward while still allowing for freedom of negotiation. He pointed out that this Government has already devalued some 21–23%.

Mr Silkin, in answer to a query, said that 2% devaluation correlated for most sectors with 2% on price-fixing because it was the intervention price that ultimately counted. But the 5% now would also be popular with the Italians and better than trying to put more on to price-fixing. Both he and Mr Howells agreed that any further devaluation and rise in incomes would be better in the autumn from a farming point of view.

Mr Pardoe concluded by agreeing the wording (below) of an amendment to the Conservative motion to be tabled the following day. He asked for Liberal names to be included as a tangible sign of Liberal–Government agreement and this was accepted.

The amendment to be tabled read:

> This House, recognising the special difficulties of the producers of pigmeat and beef, approves the action of HMG in requesting the Commission to propose an immediate devaluation of the green pound by 5% as part of a move in the course of 1978 to increase the income of such producers by not less than 10%.

C R MORRISON (Miss)
PCO
20 January 1978

Appendix 9

THE PRIME MINISTER

Dear David,   14 February 1978

Immigration and Race Relations

I am writing to amplify the suggestion which I put forward in the House during Question Time this afternoon about the best way to handle the issue of immigration and race relations. I take the view – as I made clear in the House on 7 February 1978 – that as far as possible there should be a national approach on both immigration and race relations otherwise we run a grave risk of exacerbating racial tension and hatred in our society. Since 1971 when the current legislation was enacted by Parliament there has been broad agreement and I think it essential that we should make a serious and urgent attempt to continue in this way. The alternative is that racial issues divide us. I am aware that a Select Committee of the House is currently investigating these matters but I believe that it would be in the national interest for the Party Leaders to sit down together as quickly as possible and see if we can reach agreement.

I would be ready therefore to convene a round table conference of the Leaders of the three United Kingdom political Parties to see whether we can evolve a common approach to immigration and race relations. This would enable us to exchange views on the present Act and rules and their administration, on our commitments to adhere to the pledges given both by the former Government and by the present Government, and on positive policies for the promotion of racial equality and harmony. The relevant facts and figures are readily available.

I am open to suggestions as to who should come to such a meeting but subject to agreement it might comprise the Leaders of the three United Kingdom Parties, together with the Home Secretary, Merlyn Rees, the shadow Home Secretary, Mr Whitelaw, and Mr Maudling who was the Home Secretary responsible for the present legislation under which we are operating. Our discussions would be informal and I hope that we could speedily find out what common ground exists and build on it.

I am writing similarly to Margaret Thatcher.

I am – in view of my public statement this afternoon – informing the Press that I have written to you but am not releasing the text unless you and Margaret Thatcher so wish.

Yours sincerely
Jim Callaghan

Appendix 10

Note of a Special Meeting of the Government/Liberal Consultative Committee – Room 4, House of Commons, at 7.15pm on Tuesday, 14 February 1978

Present:

Rt Hon. Michael Foot MP   Mr Alan Beith MP
Rt Hon. Tony Benn MP   Mr Richard Wainwright MP
Rt Hon. Michael Cocks MP   Mr David Penhaligon MP

Mr G W Monger (Department of Energy)
Sir Freddie Warren (Chief Whip's Office)
Mr J W Stevens

THE ELECTRICITY AND NUCLEAR MATERIALS BILL

Mr Foot opened the meeting by saying that the Government were deeply committed to the re-structuring provisions in this Bill. If there had been some misunderstandings about the background leading to the present situation whereby the Bill included these provisions, he hoped that the meeting would be able to dispel them. But in view of the discussions which had taken place with Liberal spokesmen, the Government had believed that the way was clear to proceed with the Bill.

Mr Beith said that during the past few weeks there had been intensive and helpful discussions but these had been about the DRAX B and Nuclear Materials provisions. In view of earlier information they had been given about the status of various measures in the legislative programme, the Liberals had not expected the re-structuring proposals to be included in the Bill.

Mr Foot outlined the background to the decision to amalgamate the Industry re-structuring provisions with those on DRAX B and Nuclear Materials into a single Bill, on the basis that this would be done without increasing the amount of time which would be required at the Second Reading stage. He emphasised that it was not the case that by dropping the re-structuring provisions, Second Reading time would be released for other Bills. Some extra time would be required for proceedings after Second Reading, particularly in Committee, but it was floor time which was at a premium and in this respect, time at Second Reading was of over-riding importance. But over and above the question of Parliamentary time, he believed very strongly that the discussions with all sections of the Industry were now so far advanced that it would be extremely difficult to introduce the Bill without the re-structuring proposals.

Mr Beith said that there could be further discussions on aspects in the Bill if it went ahead – but he asked why should it go ahead now?

Mr Penhaligon asked about the advantages in the proposed reorganisation and said that the onus to prove the advantages rested with those who wanted to implement the reorganisation. He could not yet see that the reorganisation would lead to a more efficient Electricity Industry producinging cheaper electricity.

Mr Benn outlined the history of the moves towards the re-structuring of the Industry over the past ten years. In 1968 Mr Roy Mason started proceedings to reorganise the CEGB but the legislation could not be completed before the 1970 General Election. The Plowden Committee then considered the matter and reported early in 1976. Since then, there had been 65 consultations with various bodies. The Industry was desperate to get reorganisation of a structure which had existed for 21 years. At the moment, it had no capacity to develop a corporate strategy towards investment or industrial relations and yet it had an investment programme of some £600 million a year and employed many thousands. There was now an expectation of a reorganisation in the Industry and the Chairman had been appointed on the basis that it would take place. The only change he had made to the Plowden recommendations was the retention of Area Boards – which was a move towards the Liberal view. The present proposals could not be regarded as a 'Power Board Bill' but the primary statute provided for flexibility and the structure of the industry could develop in that direction. It was not possible to move to a Power Board structure straight away but apart from corporate strategy and investment, no greater centralisation was now being proposed.

Mr Benn said that he believed he had met consultative requirements fully. Mr Grimond had been consulted on 13 July about proposals to reorganise the Industry which had been described to the House on 19 July. Although Mr Grimond had raised a number of points, the statement was made without Liberal disagreement. In October, there were discussions with Lord Avebury when a Liberal objection on the DRAX B proposals was resolved. The Queen's Speech included a reference to legislation providing for changes in the structure of the Electricity Industry.

Mr Wainwright commented that one of the difficulties for them was that the urgency which was now being expressed was not reflected in the earlier information which the Liberals had been given. *Mr Benn* said that the re-structuring had always been a high priority within his Department but he had to make his case with colleagues who had eventually accepted the need for a reorganisation and its inclusion in the Bill on the clear understanding that no extra Parliamentary time would be required at Second Reading.

Mr Beith pointed out that the re-structuring did not apply to Scotland; this was something of a paradox in that the South of Scotland Board supplied direct to some consumers in England. *Mr Benn* said that the responsibility for the Scottish Electricity Board rested with the Secretary of State for Scotland.

Mr Beith said that there appeared to be two levels of argument: the first concerned the priority of the re-structuring proposals within the legislative programme and the problems which would be created amongst groups within the Industry if the re-structuring was not pursued. Secondly, on the content of the Bill itself: further discussions would be needed on this but he expected that progress could be made. The Liberals were meeting tomorrow evening (Wednesday) and he would report back on the outcome of their discussions.

Mr Foot, in conclusion, emphasised that the Government could not now go into reverse on its re-structuring proposals in view of the nature and extent of the very wide-ranging discussions which had taken place. He also believed that given the present sensitive state of negotiations on pay, if we now sought to delay the re-structuring it could have very damaging consequences indeed in other fields and could even lead to accusations that the Government had misled those whom they had consulted.

In a brief reference to the Co-operative Development Agency Bill, *Mr Wainwright* said that whilst the Liberal Party Conference supported the concept of an Agency, the draft Bill which was produced was not one which the Liberals could support. Presumably because no Parliamentary time was yet available for the Bill the Liberal objections had not been pursued. *Mr Foot* undertook to look into the situation and to arrange for the matter to be discussed at a later stage.

J W Stevens
15 February 1978

Index

A figure 2 in brackets immediately after a page reference indicates that there are two separate references to the subject on that page. The following abbreviations are used:

DS – David Steel
LLA – Lib–Lab agreement
LL c.c. – Lib–Lab consultative committee
g.e. – general election
PR – proportional representation

Abortion Act, 10–11
Abse, Leo, 27
agricultural assessment, 127
agricultural credit, 182
Ahlmark, Per, 83
Aitken, Ian, 145
anti-apartheid movement, 12, 78
Atomic Energy Bill, 173
Austick, David, 13
Avebury, Eric, Lord (Eric Lubbock), 3, 10, 12, 61, 84, 90, 149–50, 176, 191

Banks, Desmond (Lord Banks), 62, 69, 154, 176, 180
Bannerman, John (later Lord Bannerman), 7
Barnett, Joel, 48, 65, 80, 81, 127, 131, 132, 134, 135, 170, 186–8
Beith, Alan: and devolution, 97; and education, 67; and LLA, 112, 114, 117; on LL c.c., 48, 55–7, 179–81, 182–4, 190–2; shadow posts, 176; wins Berwick-upon-Tweed (1973), 13; mentioned, 53, 54, 81, 143
Benn, Anthony Wedgwood: his electricity Bill, 69, 124, 126, 191–2; and European elections, 110; and Grimond, 69, 83, 154, 191; and LLA, 42, 64–5; mentioned, 114
Berwick-upon-Tweed by-election (1973), 13
Bessell, Peter, 8, 88
bill of rights, 97, 165

Bonham-Carter, Mark, 3
Booth, Albert, 42, 64–5, 86, 103, 111, 132, 154, 177
Bottomley Report, 175
Bournemouth by-election (1977), 106
Bowen, Roderic, 9
Britain, decline of, 158
British Leyland, 133, 160
Brown, George, 6
budget, Finance Bill: of 1977, 45, 47–8, 59, 168; of 1978, 127–8, 128–9, 130–2, 132–3, 133–4, 135, 136, 141–4, 145–7
bureaucracy, waste in, 160; see also national efficiency audit
Burke, Edmund, quoted, 22
business names, registration of, 170, 173
Byers, Frank (Lord Byers), 14–15, 54, 62, 69, 176

Callaghan, James (JC; PM): and devolution, 91(2), 94–5, 95–6, 97–8, 107; DS, discussions with, letters exchanged with, 48, 49–51, 52–4, 64–5, 66–7, 70(2), 71, 72, 73–6, 77–80, 84–5, 90–1, 94–5, 95–6, 97–8, 104, 107–8, 109, 110–11, 112–13, 113–14, 124, 124–6, 126, 129–31, 134, 134–7, 138–40, 141–2, 143–7, 148–9, 150–1, 155–6, 189; and European elections, 49–51, 52–4, 78, 90–1, 108, 109, 110, 110–11, 112–13, 156; and immigration,

Callaghan, James—*contd.*
124, 126, 130, 189; and Lib–Lab
overtures, 29–30, 32–5, 36–42;
mentioned, 26, 60–1, 120
CBI, 137
Ceausescu, President, 144
centre, party of, 21, 163; *see also*
parties, realignment of
Chalfont, Lord, 50
Charles, Prince, 51, 116
Civic Trust, 71
Civil Aviation Bill, 172–3, 180
class war, class-based attitudes, 160,
164
coalition, power-sharing, government
of national unity, 17–18, 23, 24–5,
156, 157
Cocks, Michael, 48, 95, 110, 112,
168, 182, 182–3
Company Law Bill, 173, 181, 184
competition policy, 75, 105, 183; *see
also* consumer protection
Conservative (Tory) Party, 160,
162
construction industry, 181
consumer protection: Liberals press
for, 64, 75, 154, 179, 183; scope
of, discussed, 105, 170, 174, 179,
183
Co-operative Development Agency,
84, 86, 125, 180, 192
Cornford, Professor James, 98
Crossman, R.H.S. (Dick), 11

Dahrendorf, Ralf, 62
Daily Express, 64, 120(2)
Daily Mail, 27, 111
Daily Mirror, 29
Daily Telegraph, 31, 41, 65
Dalyell, Tam, 4, 27
Davies, John, 141
defence, 47, 82, 117, 118, 125, 168
Desai, Morarji, 52, 141, 141–2
devaluation, *see* green pound
devolution (elected assemblies in
Scotland and Wales), 92–101; bill
of rights, 97; Callaghan
government and, 26, 27–9, 38, 47,

57, 70, 71, 72, 73, 75, 91(2), 93–
101, 107, 147–8, 169, 172, 178;
independence question, 95, 96,
107; Liberals' approach to, 27–9,
35, 37, 38, 47, 57, 61, 63, 64, 70,
71, 72(2), 73, 75, 91(2), 92–101,
107; PR and, 28, 37, 38, 64, 71, 92,
94–5, 100, 101, 147–8;
referendums, 95, 96, 97–8, 99, 107,
126
Dimbleby Lecture, 159
direct elections, *see* European
Parliament
dividend control, 146, 148
dock work scheme, 132, 149, 153
Douglas-Home, Sir Alec (Lord
Home), 4, 6, 100
Douglas-Home, William, 1
Du Cann, Edward, 185

East African Asians, 11–12, 34
Economist, The, 67
Edinburgh, Pentlands division, 3–5
Education Bill, 125 ('school
governors'), 170, 174, 179, 179–80,
182–3
electoral pact, 156–7
electoral reform, 14, 61, 63, 156–7,
161–2, 165; *see also* parties,
realignment of; political system
Electricity and Nuclear Materials
Bill, 69, 124, 126(2), 127, 128(2),
129, 130, 190–2
Electricity Supply Industry Bill, 170,
175
Ely, Isle of, by-election (1973), 13
employee shareholding, *see* profit-
sharing
employment: employment appeal,
184; Employment and Training
Bill, 170, 174; *see also*
unemployment
European Economic Community
(EEC), 19–21, 84–5
European Movement, 50
European Parliament, direct elections
to, 35, 37, 38–9, 49–51, 52–8, 64,
75, 78, 83, 86, 90–1, 103, 105,

106–7, 109–11, 112, 117, 129, 156, 167, 169, 172, 178

Evans, Moss, 123, 177

Evening News, 87

Evening Standard, 87

Ewing, Mrs Winnie, 92

expenditure, public, 30; *see also* national efficiency audit

Fenton, James, 82–3

Finance Bill, *see* budget

firemen's strike, 106, 107, 109

first-time home buyers, help for, 64, 75, 91, 169, 174, 178, 179

Foot, Michael (Lord President): and budget of 1978, 133, 141–2, 143; and devolution, 70, 71, 72(2), 94, 94–5, 96–7, 147; and European elections, 38, 54–8, 103, 112–13, 129; and legislative programme (1977–8), 77, 83–4, 86–7, 117, 118, 120, 124, 126, 128, 129, 167–8, 169–71, 172–5, 178–81, 182–5, 190–2; and LLA, establishment of, 33, 37–9, 43–7; LL c.c. chaired by, 48, 54–7, 167–8, 178–81, 182–5, 186–8, 190–2; and LLA, ending of, 136, 138; mentioned, 31, 36, 116, 123, 150

Ford Motor Co., 86, 177

Freud, Clement, 13, 63, 90, 144, 154, 176

Gaitskell, Hugh, 1, 2–3

general elections: 1964, 5; 1966, 9–10; 1970, 10, 12; Feb. 1974, 13–14, 92; Oct. 1974, 19, 93; 1979, 158

Genscher, Hans-Dietrich, 105, 120

Gifford, Andrew, 33, 108–109

Ginsburg, D., 111

Greece, Liberal party of, 123

green pound, 117, 120, 123, 186–8

Grimond, Jo: and Benn, 69, 83, 154, 191; and devolution, 28, 92, 96–7; and EEC referendum 'yes' campaign, 20; and Heath/Thorpe talks (Feb. 1974), 14–15; and Lib-

Lab overtures, 39; and LLA, 61, 62–3, 71, 112, 113; party leadership resigned by, 10; proposed as Speaker, by Peter Bessell, 8; recalled as temporary party leader, 21; in shadow administration (autumn 1977), 176; his view of Liberal Party, 1–2, 116

Guardian, The, 29, 64, 71, 122, 132, 134, 145

Hailsham, Lord, quoted, 153

Hamilton by-election (1978), 136, 138, 145

Harrison, Walter, 96

Hart, Judith, 137

Hartling, Poul, 141

Hattersley, Roy, 48, 70, 105, 154

Healey, Denis: his budgets of 1977 and 1978, *see* budget; DS, discussions with *à deux*, 128–9, 133–4, 138; his economic package of July 1977, 64, 65, 66, 69, 70–1; Pardoe, relations with, *see under* Pardoe; mentioned, 87

Heath, Edward, 14–16, 20, 26, 52, 104, 110, 137

Heffer, Eric, 36, 91

Hoggart, Simon, 29

Holme, Richard, 119

Holmes, David, 88

Home, Lord, *see* Douglas-Home, Sir Alec

Home Loans Bill, 117

Hooson, Emlyn: and European elections, 103; and LLA, 62; on LL c.c., 48, 168, 178–9, 181, 182, 186, 187; not elected Liberal leader, 10; shadow posts, 48, 176; wins Montgomery (1962), 3; mentioned, 28('Welsh colleague'), 44, 89, 109, 118('EH'), 154

House of Commons: Administration Bill, 170, 175; Committees of, 168; *see also* Parliament

Housing Finance Review, 168

Howe, Geoffrey, 144

Howells, Geraint: and devolution, 28, 98; and Land Bank, 179; and LLA, 63, 144; on LL c.c., 186–7, 188; shadow posts, 176; mentioned, 17, 81, 120, 154

Hughes, Cledwyn, 29–30, 32–3, 54

Hunt, Sir John, 78, 104–5

Hylton-Foster, Sir Harry, 8, 9

Ilford by-election (1978), 125

immigration, race relations, 90, 124, 126, 130, 133, 189

income tax: reductions in, 37, 64, 75, 79, 128, 131, 132, 133–4, 135, 137, 180; and Scottish/Welsh assemblies, 98–9

incomes policy, see pay policy

industrial relations, 160, 165

industry, aid to, 159

inflation, 26, 29, 35, 72, 74, 152

inner cities, 173–4, 178

International Monetary Fund, 29

Jackson, Peter, 11

Jenkins, Peter, 122

Jenkins, Roy, 11, 16, 20, 27, 50, 79, 105, 159, 161

Johnston, Russell, 15, 47, 61, 69–70, 72, 97, 98, 176

Jones, Elwyn, 54, 65

Jones, Hugh, 35

Jones, Jack, 87

Joseph Rowntree Social Service Trust, 98

Judd, Frank, 78

Kenya, 158

Kilbrandon Commission, 28, 92, 94

King, Dr Horace, 9

King-Murray, Ronald, 6

Kinross and West Perthshire by-election (1963), 4

Kirkwood, Archy, 60, 77, 108–9

Königswinter Conference, 43

Labour Party, 1, 2–3, 59, 160, 162

Lambsdorff, Otto, 106, 128

Land Bank, 179, 182

Land Commission, 160

Lestor, Joan, 79–80, 84

Lever, Harold: and national insurance surcharge, 141, 142(2), 143; and small businesses, 79, 80, 81, 84, 128, 129, 171; mentioned, 54

Liberal Party: Grimond's view of, 2; by-election successes, early 1960s, 3; in 1964 g.e., 5; refuses to support Labour government (1965), 8; undisciplined, 8; in 1966 g.e., 9–10; loses seats in 1970, 10, 12; by-election successes in 1970s, 13; in Feb. 1974 g.e., 13–14; in Oct. 1974 g.e., 19; 1975 assembly, 21; DS elected leader, 21–4; Brighton conference (1977), 81–5; in 1979 g.e., 158; future of, 162–6

Lib-Lab agreement/pact (LLA): origins of, 29, 30–42; consultative committee, 36–7, 43–5, 47, 48, 156, 167 (meetings of, 167–8, 178–81, 182–5, 186–9, 190–2; announced, 43; issues affecting, discussed by DS and Foot, 45–7; renewed (summer 1977), 59–76; machinery of, strengthened, 77; endorsed by party conference (autumn 1977), 83; devolution a corner-stone of, 93–4; PR for European elections not breaking point, 106–7, 112; DS presses for continuation, 113, 114–15; Scottish and Welsh Liberal support for, 120; endorsed by special assembly (Jan. 1978), 121–2; to end July 1978?, 130, 136, 136–7, 138–40, 145; without it, Labour defeated, 151; assessment of, 152–7

life peerages, 79

Lloyd George, David, quoted, 81

Local Authorities (Works) Bill, 46

Local Government Direct Labour Bill, 37

Lord President's office, 44

Lubbock, Eric, see Avebury, Eric

Macdonald, John, 88, 89
McEwen, Robin, 6
Mackie, George (Lord Mackie), 4–5, 62, 69, 69–70, 72, 98, 176
Mackintosh, John, 2, 32, 54, 67–9, 89, 94, 110
Macmillan, Harold, 1
McNally, Tom, 37, 79, 85
magistrates' courts, domestic proceedings in, 170, 175
mandate, electoral, 161
Mason, Roy, 65, 154
Mayhew, Christopher, 18, 83
Merchant Shipping Bill, 169, 174, 180–1, 184
Merrison Report, 170, 174
Methven, Sir John, 137
Millan, Bruce, 42, 64–5, 97
Miller, David, 60
Mitchell, Austen, 156
Monopolies Commission, 64
Montgomery by-election (1962), 3
Morrison, Carolyn, 77, 85
mortgages, *see* first-time home buyers; Trustee Savings Banks Bill
MPs, segregated politically, 27
Mulley, Fred, 104, 123, 154
multiple registration, 170, 175, 179, 180, 183
Murphy, Leslie, 133
Murray, Len, 72, 87, 105, 107
Muzorewa, Bishop Abel, 148

Nally, Michael, 107
national efficiency audit, 64, 91, 184–5
National Enterprise Board (NEB), 133
national insurance, 127, 128, 129, 131, 135, 141, 145–7
National Union of Mineworkers, 66
national unity, government of, *see* coalition
Nationalists, nationalism, 26; *see also* Plaid Cymru; Scottish National Party
nationalization, 37, 82, 152–3
New Statesman, 82–3

News of the World, 72
Nigeria, 78
North Sea oil, 79, 98, 125
Northern Ireland Judicature Bill, 170, 174
Nott, John, 104

Observer, The, 107
Occupational Pensions Schemes Bill, 46, 154 ('pension funds'), 180, 184
office development, permits for, 46
Official Secrets Acts, 64, 75, 170, 174–5, 179
oil: North Sea, 79, 98, 125; participation agreements, 173
O'Kennedy, Michael, 110
Orme, Stanley, 41, 64–5, 111, 180
Orpington by-election (1962), 3
Outer Circle Policy Group, 98
Owen, David, 52, 54, 57, 87, 109, 110, 123, 148

Pardoe, John: Callaghan on, 113, 114, 142; his character, 135, 154; and EEC referendum campaign, 20; and Healey, 1978 budget, 69, 70–1, 103–4, 112, 118, 127–8, 129, 131–2, 132–3, 134, 135, 137, 142, 143, 145–7, 154; joins Liberals from Labour, 2; and Lib–Lab overtures, 36, 38, 39(2); and LLA, 62, 71, 117; on LL C.C., 44, 48, 55–7, 167–8, 178, 181, 182–5, 186–8; not elected party leader, 21–4; and pay Policy, 64, 66, 70–1, 111–12, 118, 146–7; and PR for Scotland, 94, 95, 136, 138; shadow post, 176; mentioned, 10, 19, 30, 59, 120, 149, 173
Parliament: stability in, due to LLA, 152; *see also* House of Commons; parties
Parry, Terry, 107
Participation Agreements Bill, 173
parties, realignment of, 1–2, 3, 16, 18, 62, 162; bi-party government, 152–3; centre party, 21, 163; *see also* political system

pay policy, prices and incomes policy: DS and Foot discuss prices, 45; Healey and Pardoe discussions, 70–1, 112, 118, 147; Heath government, 13; Liberals press for pay policy, 35, 61, 66, 74, 107, 177; need for, 159, 165–6

Peart, Fred, 54, 65

peers, Liberal, 15, 43, 69

Penhaligon, David, 39, 48, 61, 71, 72, 86, 118('DP'), 154, 176, 191

pension funds, trade union nominees on, see Occupational Pensions Schemes Bill

pensioners, Christmas bonus for, 181

Pentlands, DS and, 3–5

petrol tax, 47–8, 49, 63, 82, 127, 132, 168

Pincher, Chapman, 120(2), 121

Plaid Cymru, 92; see also Nationalists

police pay, 89–90

political system, British, 158–66; see also electoral reform; Parliament; parties, realignment of

Post Office, industrial democracy in, 45–6, 49, 167, 169, 174, 179, 181, 184

Powell, Enoch, 110

power-sharing, see coalition

Power Stations (Financial Arrangements) Bill, 173, 180

prices and incomes, see pay policy

Prior, James, 144

Private Eye, 148

profit-sharing, employee shareholding: a distinctive Liberal policy, 153, 160, 170–1; Liberals press for, 64, 75, 77, 78, 80, 90, 117, 170–1, 180, 183; in 1978 budget, 127; popular among Labour voters, 79; stressed at Brighton conference, 82–3; TUC lobbied on, 105

proportional representation (PR): in devolution proposals, 28, 37, 38, 64, 71, 92, 94–5, 100, 101, 147–8; in elections to European Parliament (q.v.), regional list scheme, 37, 38–9, 49–51, 52–8, 64, 78, 83, 86, 90–1, 103, 105, 106–7, 109–11, 112, 129, 156; need for, 161

public enquiries, legal assistance at, 75

Public Lending Right, 170, 175

race relations, see immigration

Raphael, Adam, 107

Rees, Merlyn: DS, discussions with, 89–90, 133; and European elections, 54, 55, 57, 58; on LL c.c., 44, 48, 54, 55, 187; mentioned, 109

referendums: on devolution, 95, 96, 97–8, 99, 107, 126; on EEC, 19–21

refugees, 141

regional list, see under proportional representation

Rhodesia, 148, 165

Ripon by-election (1973), 13

Robinson, Kenneth, 11

Rochdale by-election (1972), 13

Rodgers, Bill, 32, 32–3, 48, 54, 154

Ross, Stephen, 17, 46, 61, 154, 176

Roxburgh, Selkirk and Peebles constituency: DS and, 4–7

Rundle, Stanley, 107

Saffron Walden by-election (1977), 63, 65, 66, 67

school governors, see Education Bill

Scotland: elected assembly for, see devolution; home rule for, 92; independence for, 95, 96, 107

Scott, Norman, 21, 87–9, 90

Scottish Liberal Party, 60–1, 120, 145

Scottish National Party, 29, 92; see also Nationalists

seat belts, 170

second home owners, see multiple registration

Seear, Nancy, Baroness, 62, 69, 84, 86, 132, 154, 176, 177

self-employed, 63, 64, 180
services pay, 135
Shelter, 12
shipbuilding, redundancies in, 46, 173, 178
Shore, Peter, 111, 154
Silkin, John, 11, 154, 179, 186-8
Silkin, Sam, 149
Sinclair, Sir George, 11
small businesses, help for: Lever works on, 79, 80, 128, 129; Liberals not credited for Lever appointment, 80, 81, 84, 171; Liberals press for, 63, 64, 74, 79, 180
Smith, Cyril: appointed chief whip, 19; his character, 29, 69; employment spokesman, 49, 83; Lib-Lab overtures proposed by, 29; and LLA, 61, 62, 69, 83, 113, 120, 121; on LL C.C., 49; and national insurance surcharge, 143, 144; wins Rochdale (1972), 13; mentioned, 44, 64, 154
Smith, John, 70, 72, 94, 97, 98, 99-100, 101
social policy, 166
Speaker, election of, 8-9
Stetchford by-election (1977), 33
Steed, Michael, 126
Steel, Billy, 32
Steel, David (*to avoid repetition, this entry does not include full particulars of the issues and personalities of the Lib–Lab period, which will be found under their own headings elsewhere in the index*): abortion, his private member's Bill on, 10-11; Anti-Apartheid Movement, President of, 12; BBC Scotland, works for, 5; Callaghan, his relations with, 34, 53, 155; chief whip, appointment as, 12, 19; Edinburgh (Pentlands), prospective candidate for, 3-5; and EEC referendum campaign, 19-21; first public speech to electorate, 1; foreign affairs spokesman,

appointment as, 19; Grimond, first meeting with, 1; Kinross by-election, Liberal deputy agent in, 4; LLA, his assessment of, 152-6; marries, 3; MP, election as, 7; 1970 g.e., narrow majority in, 10; not an early riser, 20; 'his' office, overcrowded, 77, 80-1; Pardoe, his view of, 135, 154-5; party leader, election as, 21-4; political system, parties, his views on, 156-7, 158-66; resignation threat, 106-7, 108, 114; Roxburgh, Selkirk and Peebles, candidate for, 4-7; Scottish Liberal Party, assistant secretary of, 3; Shelter, Chairman of Scottish Committee of, 12; time-wasting functions avoided by, 51
Steel, Judy, 3-4, 51-2, 114
steel industry, 125, 129, 129-30, 159
Stowe, Ken, 34, 37, 39-41, 51, 145
Sutton and Cheam by-election (1972), 13

taxation: hotel construction allowances, 127; tax credits, 166; *see also* income tax; petrol tax; VAT
Taylor Report, *see* Education Bill
teachers: probationary, 181; unemployment among, 75, 90
Tennant, James, 4
Thatcher, Mrs Margaret: and DS, 72, 116, 125; and Heath, 26, 104; and immigration, 124, 126, 130; and mandates, 161; no confidence motion tabled by (March 1977), 30-1, 42; and refugees, 141; and services pay, 135
Thorn, Gaston, 50, 105-6
Thorpe, Jeremy: appoints DS chief whip, 12; and European elections, 53, 54-7, 110, 167; Heath talks (Feb. 1974), 14-16; and LLA, 61-2, 71; on LL C.C., 55-7; as party

Thorpe, Jeremy—*contd.*
  leader, 10, 13, 14–16, 18–19, 21;
  and Scott case, 21, 148, 149–50;
  shadow posts, 176; mentioned, 10,
  51, 118
Times, The, 66, 132
Tordoff, Geoff, 35–6, 63
Torrington by-election (1958), 3
transport, rural, 47–8, 127, 154, 168
Transport Bill, 172
Transport and General Workers
  Union, 66, 86, 177
Tribunites, 59
Trudeau, Pierre, 50
Trustee Savings Banks Bill, 173,
  180–1, 184
Tyler, Paul, 17

Ulster Unionists, 110
unemployment, 26, 74; among
  teachers, 75, 90; among young
  people, school leavers, 64, 74–5,
  103, 180; *see also* employment

Varley, Eric, 49, 130, 154
VAT, 63, 82, 134
vehicle excise duty, 47, 168

Wainwright, Richard: and Leyland,
  133 ('RW'); and LLA, 61, 117; on
  LL C.C., 191, 192; and Post Office,
  49; shadow posts, 49, 176; and
  steel industry, 130; mentioned, 39,
  81, 84, 143, 154
Waldheim, Dr Kurt, 133
Wales: elected assembly for, *see*
  devolution; independence for, 95,
  96, 107
Warren, Sir Freddie, 48, 178
Welsh Liberal Party, 120
Wigoder, Basil (Lord Wigoder), 62,
  176
Williams, Shirley, 54, 67, 90, 183
Wilson, Harold, 2–3, 9, 16, 19, 87,
  137–8
Winstanley, Michael (Lord
  Winstanley), 61, 176